Recovery from Gambling and Alcohol Addiction: 2 Books in 1 - Master your Brain to obtain Freedom from Alcoholism and Gambling addiction issues.

by Rick Conall

Table of Contents:

Book 1: Alcoholism and Recovery

Introduction:

As per the American Medical Association, alcoholism is a condition marked by a severe disability that is directly linked with chronic and inappropriate use of alcohol.
Disability can include physiological or social impotence. Psychologically speaking, alcohol abuse has less to do with how much someone is going to drink, and more to do with what actually occurs when they drink. The truth is that alcohol is sometimes abused because it provides a very enticing promise in the beginning. Most people get more comfortable with moderate intoxication. We feel more concerned about it. Any issues that pre-exist appear to fade into the background. You can use alcohol to boost a good mood or to alter a bad mood. Alcohol helps the drinker to feel relaxed at first, without any emotional costs. It is a significant challenge to overcome alcohol addiction. Alcoholism is often accepted as the drinker's friend. If somebody is a functional alcoholic, they are going to see it as something that is not just the big deal. In fact, in the most insidious ways, alcoholism can take over someone's life. In most cases, alcohol is legal and socially acceptable, as opposed to heroin or cocaine addiction. This means no one will say anything if someone goes out for a drink (or five days a week) every night. That makes it as difficult to quit alcohol as to quit smoking. Because you don't have to make special attempts to use your drug of choice, it's convenient to do it all the time. Alcohol is everywhere,

so it's like buying the food. The fact is that it's always next to you.

Due to advancements in modern medicine, it is easier than ever to detoxify alcohol if you want to stop drinking. Not more than one alcoholic drink per day is recommended by the National Institutes of Health for women and two for men, which it considers to be moderate drinking. You have the risk of a variety of medical problems beyond that, including liver, pancreas, heart, and nerve damage. Even responsible drinkers should watch their alcohol consumption closely, and it is time to do something about it if it is consistently going beyond the recommended maximum. If you want to stop drinking without AA or treatment, start with a consultation with your health care provider; your doctor will place your drinking in a medical context that is relevant to your individual health concerns. Additionally, there are several approaches that you can use to help you minimize your alcohol consumption or stop drinking entirely, ensuring that you live a healthy and fulfilling life.

When you will get started with recovery from the addiction to alcoholism, at that stage, you may face various problems, because it becomes a need of your body. Addiction lives in the circuitry of your brain it's not a personal weakness. The more frequently you turn on your paths of pleasure, the less pleasure you feel over time. To feel those happy drinks, the brain will be looking for stronger and stronger triggers. After so much repetition, your brain becomes accustomed to the stimulus, and over time you're so used to it that you've got to have your fix to work.

You can start to recover from alcoholism by withdrawing and detoxing. Exercise may also cut the alcoholism. There are many alcohol rehab centers where you get treatment. After a complete medication and with the help of your doctors and medical staff you can overcome this addiction. When you are going to quit alcoholism, the only thing you miss is the hangover tomorrow. It's a decision you're never going to regret. Sometimes you may be dealing with it, but you will never regret it.

There are the benefits of not being an alcoholic, you have a healthier lifestyle, you feel fresh all day. You have a focus on your work and have a good relationship with your loved ones.

Chapter 1: What are the Facts about Alcoholism?

Alcoholism is when the use of alcohol is no longer controlled and alcohol is compulsively consumed, the negative ramifications and emotional distress when not drinking can be caused by alcohol consumption disorder. Alcohol consumption disorder is a chronic, persistent condition diagnosed based on a patient that fits the requirements specified in the Alcoholic Diagnosis.

In order to be diagnosed with alcoholism, individuals must meet any of the criteria listed below.

- Use alcohol in higher quantities or with a daily routine.
- Alcohol use is unable to be reduced despite a desire to do so.
- It takes a great deal of time to recover from the effects of alcohol.
- Cravings or a strong alcohol appetite.

- Due to alcohol use, I am unable to fulfill major obligations at home, at work, or at school.
- Continued interpersonal or social issues likely to be caused by alcohol use.
- Giving up personal, work, or recreational activities that previously used to enjoy, due to alcohol use.
- Use of alcohol in conditions of physical danger (such as driving or operating machinery).
- Continued alcohol abuse despite the presence of an alcohol-related psychological or physical problem.
- Tolerance (i.e., drinking increasingly large amounts of alcohol or more frequently in order to achieve the desired effect).
- I am developing withdrawal symptoms when attempts are made to stop alcohol use.

Women who have no more than three drinks on a given day and no more than seven drinks per week are at low risk for developing AUD (AUD is a chronic brain disease caused by alcohol abuse), according to the National Institute on Alcohol Abuse & Alcoholism (NIAAA). For people, no more than four drinks on a given day and no more than 14 per week are described as this low-risk range.

1.1 Alcoholism facts

According to National Survey 2017, Drug Use and Health (NSDUH), 51% of the population aged 12 years and older reported binge drinking during the previous month.

Five or more male drinks define binge drinking and four or more female drinks over the past month on at least one day; heavy alcohol consumption indicates five or more days of binge drinking over the past month. Three Most binge drinking occurs among people aged 18 34 and is twice as common among men as women. One in six adults' binges drinks about four times a month. Over the past month, 5.3% of 12-17-year-olds reported binge drinking, with 0.7% reporting heavy alcohol consumption over the past month. While not everyone who binges drinks has an AUD, binge drinking can be a major risk factor for AUD. The NSDUH reports that in 2017, over 14 million people aged 12 years and older had an AUD, with AUD occurring in 7% of males and 3.8% of females aged 12 years and older.4 In 2015, 47.0% of deaths from alcohol-related liver disease in people aged 12 years and older were due to drug use. Six In addition to these deaths from alcohol-related liver disease, alcohol-related deaths are attributed to alcohol use. Alarmingly, according to 2015 figures from the Centers for Disease Control and Prevention, every year, more than 2,200 people die from alcohol poisoning, with Three out of Four deaths originating in men and non- Hispanic white adults aged 35,64.7 An average of 6 people die every day as a result of alcohol poisoning or so much consumption that the body is overwhelmed and the critical areas of the disease are compromised.

1.2 Alcoholism is hereditary

According to the DSM-5, alcoholism is believed to have a large heritable component, with genetic factors attributable to between 40 and 60 percent of the risk variance. Though, there is no cut-and-dry equation for alcoholism explanations. It is a multi-faceted and nuanced disease, so while someone may inherit a predisposition to a disorder, biology does not completely decide a person's outcome.

1.3 Causes of Alcoholism

No single cause of alcoholism exists. In addition, in the creation of alcohol addiction, there are hundreds of risk factors that play a role. In each adult, these risk factors interact differently, leading to disorders of alcohol use in some and not others.

The development of addiction is affected by both internal and external causes. Genetics, psychological conditions, personality, personal choice, and history of drinking include internal factors. External factors include family, climate, ethnicity, social and cultural norms, gender, health, and employment status.

The sheer diversity of factors that could affect the development of alcohol addiction makes it virtually impossible to predict exactly whether any person will develop alcoholism. While it is an individual's personal decision whether to start drinking or not, much research suggests that when drinking starts, the development of addiction is beyond the control of that individual.IT is also true that when someone becomes an alcoholic or not, there can be no single factor or group of factors affecting a person's probability of alcohol consumption. Individuals with depression, bipolar disorder, and social anxiety, for instance, are much more likely to develop alcoholism. More than 40 percent of bipolar patients misuse or are alcohol dependent, and about 20 percent of anxiety patients abuse or are alcohol dependent.

Many psychologically ill individuals turn to alcohol as a way to cope with their disease. Some with schizophrenia, for example, claim that alcohol "quiets" the voices in their head, while others with depression claim that alcohol elevates their mood. This is particularly common in people who were not treated with drugs or had unpleasant side effects. However, most psychological disorders reduce an individual's ability to interpret their reality of drinking or overlook threats and signs of alarm.

Chapter 2: Causes and Effects of Alcoholism

Problems of alcohol vary in severity from mild to life threatening, affecting the individual, the family, and society in many ways. Despite focusing on illegal abuse drugs like cocaine, alcohol remains America's number one drug problem. Nearly seventeen million adults in the U.S are alcohol-dependent or have other alcohol-related issues, and about 88,000 people die from alcohol-related preventable causes.

2.1 Alcoholism

The most commonly used drug in adolescents is alcohol. Thirty-five percent of teenagers had at least one drink at 15 years of age. Although it is illegal, in the past month, about 8.7 million people aged 12 to 20 had a drink, and this age group accounted for 11% of all alcohol consumed in the U.S. Alcohol is responsible for nearly 189,000 emergency room visits and 4,300 deaths annually among underage teens.

Withdrawal is much more dangerous for those physically dependent on alcohol than withdrawal from heroin or other substances. Under the classification of a drug use disorder, alcohol abuse and alcohol dependency are now grouped together.

- What was previously referred to as alcohol abuse refers to excessive or problematic use with one or more of the following:
- Failure to fulfill major obligations at work, at school or at home
- Recurring use in hazardous situations (such as driving a car or operating machinery)
- Legal problems
- Continued use of alcohol despite medical, social, family or interpersonal problems caused by or caused by alcohol abuse;

How many drinks make an Alcoholic?

Previously referred to as alcohol dependence; this aspect of alcohol use disorder refers to a more serious type of alcohol use disorder and involves excessive or maladaptive use resulting intolerance.

2.2 What Causes Alcoholism

Not well established is the cause of alcoholism. There is increasing evidence of this disease's genetic and biological predisposition. First-degree alcohol-use disorder relatives are four to seven times more likely than the general population to develop alcoholism. Research has involved a gene (D2 dopamine receptor gene) that may increase a person's chance of developing alcoholism when inherited in a specific form.

A variety of factors typically contributes to the development of an alcohol problem. Social factors such as family, friends, and culture impact, and alcohol accessibility, and psychological factors such as elevated stress levels, insufficient coping mechanisms, and encouragement of alcohol use by other drinkers may lead to alcoholism. Often, when the disease progresses, the factors contributing to initial alcohol use may differ from those that sustain it.

Although it may not be causative, there are twice as many people dependent on alcohol. One study showed that one-third of men aged 18-24 met the alcohol dependence criteria and those beginning to drink before age 15 are four times more likely to develop alcohol dependence. Men are more likely to drink binge or drink heavily. We are also more likely to engage in activities that damage themselves or others such as alcoholrelated violence, use other substances such as marijuana and cocaine, have sex with six or more partners, and mostly receive Ds and Fs in grades at school.

2.3 Alcoholism Signs and Symptoms

It is often more diagnosed by behaviors and adverse functioning effects than by specific medical symptoms. Physiological (tolerance and withdrawal symptoms) are just two of the diagnostic criteria.

- Tolerance (need for more alcohol to achieve the desired effect or effect). According to government sources, parental alcoholism is at the root of many family issues such as divorce, spousal abuse, child abuse, and neglect, as well as dependence on public assistance and criminal behaviors.

- The vast majority of alcoholics go unrecognized by physicians and healthcare professionals. This is largely due to the tendency of the person with alcohol use disorder to hide the amount and rate of drinking, deny problems caused or exacerbated by drinking, there is a progressive progression of the disease and effects on the body, and the body has the ability to adapt up to a point to higher alcohol levels.

- Family members often dismiss or diminish alcohol problems and unintentionally contribute to the persistence of addiction through well-meaning activities such as shielding (alcohol dependence) from negative effects of drinking or taking on family or economic obligations. Drinking activity is often withheld from loved ones and experts in health care.

- Individuals with alcohol use disorder are often denied excess alcohol intake when they are challenged. Alcoholism is a complex disorder and is often affected by both the temperament of the alcoholism sufferer and other factors. Signs and symptoms of a drinking problem also vary from person to person. There are certain symptoms and signs that suggest that someone may have an alcohol problem, including fatigue, repeated drops, bruises of different ages, blackouts, chronic depression, anxiety, irritability, interruption or absence at work or school, job loss, divorce or breakup, financial difficulties, excessive intoxication or behavior, weight loss, or frequent car co-operation.

- Intoxication symptoms include slurred speech, reduced inhibitions, and judgment, lack of muscle control, coordination problems, confusion, or memory or concentration problems. Continued drinking causes increased levels of blood alcohol (BAC), and high levels of BAC can lead to breathing problems, coma, and even death.

- A drinking problem is actually signs, and symptoms often vary from person to person. There are certain symptoms and signs indicating that someone may have an alcohol problem, including fatigue, repeated drops, bruises of different ages, blackouts, chronic depression, anxiety, irritability, agitation or lack of restraint, failure or absence at work or school, job loss, divorce or breakup, financial difficulties, excessive intoxication or behavior, self-reliance.

- Chronic alcohol abuse signs and symptoms include medical conditions such as pancreatitis, gastritis, (liver) cirrhosis, neuropathy, anemia, cerebellar atrophy, alcoholic cardiomyopathy (heart disease), encephalopathy of Wernicke (abnormal brain function), dementia of Korsakoff, central pontine myelinolysis (brain degeneration), epilepsy, depression, fatigue, delusions, peptide.

- Children of alcohol-dependent parents are at increased risk of alcohol abuse, abuse of drugs, behavioral problems, violent behavior, anxiety disorders, compulsive behavior, and mood disorders compared to children in families without alcoholism. The risk of psychiatric disorders and suicide is higher for alcoholics. We also feel guilt, shame, isolation, anxiety, and depression, especially when their use of alcohol leads to significant losses (e.g., work, relationships, reputation, economic security, or physical health). Many medical problems are caused by alcoholism and the poor adherence of the alcoholic to medical treatment or made worse by it.

2.4 Seek Medical Care

People who drink alcohol to the degree that it interferes with their personal, physical or mental health should visit a doctor to discuss the issue. The big problem is that denial plays a big part in alcoholism. As a result, alcoholics seldom pursue voluntary professional assistance.

A family member or boss sometimes persuades or pressures the intoxicated person to seek medical treatment. Even if a person with addiction refuses treatment because of family, employer, or professional medical stress, he or she can benefit from it. Treatment may help this individual gain motivation to change the issue of alcohol.

Alcohol causes 40% of motor vehicle deaths, 70% of drownings, 50% of suicides, and up to 40% of violent crimes, including killing, theft, assault, and child and spousal abuse.

Immediately after alcohol has led to an accident, it is important to receive emergency care. This is important because someone who is intoxicated may not reliably assess the severity of the injury they have sustained or inflicted. For example, an intoxicated person may not notice a fractured neck vertebra (broken neck) until it is too late, and there has been paralysis.

In the emergency department of a hospital, several alcohol-related conditions require immediate evaluation.

- The removal of alcohol needs immediate care. A person usually goes through four phases when withdrawing from alcohol: tremulousness (shakes), seizures, hallucinations, and delirium tremors (DTs). Such phases are listed in more detail; the individual will display a tremor (shakiness) of his hands and legs during the tremulous phase. If the person stretches out his or her hand and tries to keep it still, you can see that.

Anxiety and anxiety also follow this symptom.

- The seizures can follow the tremulous phase. These are usually severe seizures in which the entire body shakes uncontrollably, the person loses consciousness and may lose control over his or her bladder or intestines. If you see someone who has a seizure, call 911 first. Then try to put the person on one side so that they don't inhale into their lungs vomit or secretions. Protect the head or other body parts of the person from uncontrollably knocking on the floor or against other potentially harmful objects, if possible. Do not put anything in the mouth of the patient while a seizure occurs.

- Most people suffering from late stages of severe alcohol withdrawal suffer from hallucinations. The most common type of hallucination encountered during the withdrawal of alcohol is visual hallucinations. People are going to "ear" bugs or worms that crawl on or over their skin on walls. This is often associated with tactile hallucinations (feeling) in which alcoholics feel insects crawling on their skin. Formalization is called this phenomenon. Although less common than the other forms of hallucinations, auditory (hearing) hallucinations may also occur during withdrawal.

- Delirium tremens (DTs) is the most serious level of alcohol withdrawal and is a medical emergency. Approximately 5 percent of people who withdraw from DTs experience alcohol. The disorder usually occurs within 72 hours of stopping drinking, but may occur up to 7 to 10 days later. This stage's hallmark is a deep delirium (confusion). People are awake but confused to a great extent. This is followed by anxiety, paranoia, vomiting, hallucinations, rapid heart rate, and high blood pressure (beliefs that have no basis in reality). This condition is associated with a death rate of 5 percent, even with adequate medical treatment.

- Another alcohol-related disorder for which emergency medical attention should be obtained is alcoholic ketoacidosis (AKA). AKA often begins within two to four days of an alcoholic has stopped drinking alcohol, fluids, and food, often due to gastritis or pancreatitis. Not uncommonly, syndromes of AKA and withdrawal of alcohol are seen concurrently. Nausea, nausea, abdominal pain, fatigue, and an acetone-like odor on the breath of the person describe AKA. This happens when carbohydrate fuel stores and water have depleted the alcohol dependent person. The body starts metabolizing ("burn") fat and protein for energy into ketone bodies. Ketone bodies are poisons that accumulate in the blood, increase their acidity, and make the person feel even more ill, perpetuating a vicious cycle.

- Depression of alcohol use is frequently related to other psychiatric disorders such as anxiety, depression, bipolar disorder, and psychosis. Also associated with a reduced level of sound judgment when intoxicated, these psychological disorders lead to suicides and suicide attempts by alcoholdependent individuals. A person who tried to commit suicide or is considered to have a significant or imminent risk of suicide should be taken to a hospital's emergency department immediately.

2.5 Risks of Heavy Drinking

How do professionals in health care diagnose alcoholism?

Drug use disorder diagnosis is usually made by examining the actions of the person unless the person shows symptoms of withdrawal or organ damage that are clearly the result of drug use.

Alcohol use disorder is defined as alcohol consumption to the point where, from an occupational, social, or health point of view, it interferes with the life of the individual. It follows that different people can interpret behaviors shown by a person with this condition in different ways. This often makes it somewhat difficult to diagnose alcoholism.

- In order to identify people at risk for alcoholism, several screening tests are routinely used. Usually, such tests consist of one or more questionnaires. The Michigan Alcohol Screening Test (MAST), the CAGE questionnaire, and the TACE questionnaire are widely used tests.
- The Michigan Alcohol Diagnostic test (MAST) is a 22-question quiz that is often used in clinical guidance.
- For example, the CAGE questionnaire asks four questions. "Yes," responses to two or more of these questions suggest a high risk of alcoholism.
- Did you feel you were supposed to cut back on your drink?
- Have you been bothered by people criticizing your drink?
- Did you feel bad about your drinking or guilty?
- Have you ever had to drink for the first time in the morning?
- It is identical to the TACE questionnaire. The poses four questions as well. The more "yes" a person has to answer these questions, the higher the person's probability of excessive drinking.

- Are you taking more than two drinks to get you up?
- Have you been bothered by people criticizing your drink?
- Have you ever thought that your drink should be cut down?
- Have you ever had a drink to calm your nerves in the morning (Eye-opener)?

A doctor can draw blood to assess your liver function, test for anemia, and/or electrolyte imbalance (levels of blood chemistry). Sometimes, alcoholics have elevated liver function tests that show damage to the liver. The most sensitive liver function test is gamma-glutamyl transferase (GGT). After a few weeks of excess alcohol consumption, it can be elevated. Alcohol-dependent individuals may also have anemia (low number of blood cells), As well as anomalies in electrolytes, including low potassium, low magnesium, low calcium.

The initial clinic appointment also causes clinical or surgical alcohol consumption complications. Based on the symptoms (e.g., stomach pain, heart failure, cessation of alcohol, or cirrhosis), the doctor will conduct and prescribe additional tests in those cases.

2.6 Remedies for Alcoholism?

Specialists trained in addiction medicine best treat alcoholism. Doctors and other healthcare workers with such specialized training and experience are best suited for managing alcohol withdrawal and alcohol-related medical and mental disorders.

Due to complications from alcohol withdrawal syndrome, home therapy without supervision by a trained professional can be life-threatening. Normally, after reducing or halting alcohol consumption, an alcoholic may start experiencing alcohol withdrawal six to eight hours.

There are several levels of alcohol treatment available. Medically controlled hospital-based detoxification and rehabilitation programs are used with medical and psychiatric problems for more severe cases of addiction. Medically regulated services for detoxification and recovery are used for people who are dependent on alcohol and do not need more closely supervised medical care. The aim of detoxification is to secure the alcohol addicted person's withdrawal from alcohol and to help him or her into a recovery treatment program (rehab). A rehabilitation program aims to help the client understand the state of addiction, continue to develop sober living skills, and engage in ongoing programs of care and selfhelp. The majority of detoxification programs last only a few days. Most rehabilitation programs that are managed or monitored medically last less than two weeks. Longterm rehabilitation programs, day treatment programs, or outpatient programs support most alcoholics. Such services provide counseling, rehabilitation, addressing issues that lead to or result from addiction, and learning skills over time to treat alcoholism.

These are the abilities include but are not limited to:

- Identifying and controlling what leads to alcohol cravings' triggers.
- I am resisting social pressure to engage in substance use.
- I am changing healthcare habits and lifestyle (e.g., improving diet and sleep hygiene and avoiding high-risk people, places, and events).

Learning to challenge alcoholic thinking (e.g., thinking like this).

2.7 Treatment for Alcoholism

A group of clinicians is often needed to treat an alcoholic. The doctor usually plays a key role in clinical recovery and promoting admission into care, but others are regularly required beyond initial management (e.g., counselors for addiction, social workers, behavioral specialist doctors, family psychologists, and pastoral counselors).

Alcohol rehabilitation can be split into three stages. Initially, the person must be stabilized medically. Next, a detoxification cycle must be performed, followed by longterm abstinence and recovery.

- Stabilization: Alcoholism is associated with many medical and surgical problems, but only alcohol withdrawal stabilization and alcoholic ketoacidosis are discussed here.
- Withdrawal of alcohol is treated with oral or intravenous (IV) hydration along with drugs that reverse the symptoms of withdrawal of alcohol.

  The sedative class also called benzodiazepines such as lorazepam (Ativan), diazepam (Valium), and chlordiazepoxide (Librium), is the most common cause of drugs used to treat symptoms of alcohol withdrawal. These can be given by injection, orally, or by IV. Also, Diazepam comes as a rectal assumption. Chlordiazepoxide usually takes longer than diazepam or lorazepam to have an effect and is, therefore, less widely used in emergencies of withdrawal. Pentobarbital is another medicine that is sometimes used to treat withdrawal from alcohol. It has a similar effect to benzodiazepines but is more likely to slow down breathing, making it less appealing to this application. Occasionally, the agitated and frustrated person may need to be restrained physically until it becomes calm and coherent.

- IV fluids and carbohydrates are treated for alcoholic ketoacidosis. This is usually done in the type of sugar-containing IV-administered fluid until the patient can begin to drink and eat liquids.

People with alcoholism should receive additional thiamine (vitamin B1), either by injection, injection, or mouth. Thiamine levels are often low in people dependent on alcohol, and deficiency of this important vitamin could lead to Wernicke's encephalopathy, a disorder initially characterized by eyes looking in different directions. When thiamine is administered in a timely manner, it can completely reverse this potentially devastating disease. Thiamine is usually given as an injection in the emergency setting. Magnesium and folate (a vitamin) are also often given to people with alcoholism.

- Detoxification: Avoid alcohol consumption at this point. For an alcohol-dependent person, this is very difficult, requires extreme discipline, and usually requires extensive support. It often takes place in a hospital setting where there is no alcohol available. In the treatment of alcohol withdrawal, the patient is treated with the same drugs, namely benzodiazepines. During detoxification, the medication is carefully measured to prevent symptoms of physical withdrawal and then gradually diminished until there are no symptoms of physical withdrawal. It takes a few days to a week. As physician-assisted ambulatory detoxification has become popular, coverage for inhospital detoxification may become more difficult.

- Rehabilitation: Short-and long-term residential programs aim to help people who rely more heavily on alcohol develop non-drinking skills, build a recovery support system, and work on ways to prevent them from drinking (relapse).

- Less than four weeks of short-term programs. Longer services last from one month to one year or more and are often called sober-living facilities. These are formal services that provide counseling,

- instruction, development in skills, and help to develop a long-term plan to prevent a recurrence.
- Ambulance therapy (individually, in groups, and/or with families) may be used as a primary treatment tool or as a "step-down" for individuals as they emerge from a residential or formal day program.

  Ambulance counseling can provide alcohol and recovery education, help people learn skills and self-image not to drink, and identify early signs of potential recurrence.

- In outpatient treatment clinics, there are several very effective individual treatments provided by professional counselors. Twelve-step facilitation therapy, motivational improvement therapy, and cognitive-behavioral coping skills are these treatments.

Alcoholics Anonymous (AA) is a well-known self-help program. Other self-help programs (such as Women for Sobriety, Rational Recovery, and SMART Recovery) allow alcoholics to stop drinking and remain self- sufficient.

Medications

What medications can be used in alcohol treatment? Many drugs are available to help the patient abstain from alcohol use.

Perhaps disulfiram (Antabuse) is the oldest and one of the most widely used medicines. It interferes with the metabolism of alcohol, resulting in a metabolite, which makes the person very uncomfortable and nauseated when alcohol is consumed. The biggest problem with disulfiram is that in order to drink alcohol, people often stop taking the medication. Disulfiram is available as an implantable device implanted under the skin to overcome this problem. Fatalities were reported when people taking disulfiram ingested large amounts of alcohol. Disulfiram has been associated with various types of neurological conditions, including optic neuritis (optic nerve inflammation), which can result in vision impairment and eye pain.

Certain drugs used to avoid alcohol relapse include naltrexone, acamprosate (Campral), and a class of antidepressants called selective serotonin reuptake inhibitors (SSRIs). Several researchers suggest that the most effective drugs tested seem to be naltrexone and acamprosate and that SSRIs are not as effective. Disulfiram appears to have a positive effect on maintaining an alcohol-free lifestyle, but it appears that the magnitude of this effect is rather limited. Naltrexone is, therefore, gradually being used. Studies suggest that alcoholics who consume less alcohol while on naltrexone have less serious relapses relative to non-alcoholics. Acamprosate is sometimes used to control the addiction caused by the chemical imbalance in the brain. It has been effective in helping people abstain from alcohol compared to placebo (sugar pills). Both medications are generally recommended to be used in combination with treatment for addiction.

Is follow-up Needed after Alcoholism Treatmen

The person with alcohol use disorder must first decide to stop using alcohol. Without such a determination, it is unlikely to achieve long-term sobriety. To prevent an impulsive relapse, the home of the patient should be alcohol-free.

The person should be involved in a group or therapy program for social support. It is also important to avoid social situations that promote alcohol consumption.

It can all be helpful to use cognitive behavioral therapy, aversion therapy, family therapy, and group psychotherapy.

When medication is prescribed to help maintain sobriety, the patient must follow a strict schedule to take the medication. It is essential to meet a counselor. When the urge to relapse is intense, the patient should contact a member of his or her support group immediately and address the urge to resist it.

Is It Possible to Prevent Alcoholism?

Abstinence is the best way to prevent alcoholism. Before becoming dependent on the drug, you must first have access to alcohol. A strong alcohol family history is a warning that you are at an increased risk of becoming alcohol-dependent. Increased awareness of such a risk factor can help change your alcohol consumption attitude. A good system of social services and early medical or psychiatric intervention can also help prevent alcohol consumption that is so typical of addiction from worsening.

What Is the Prognosis of Alcoholism?

Remaining free of alcohol is a very difficult task for most people with drug use disorders. After detoxification, individuals who do not seek help tend to have a high rate of relapse.

Higher rates of frustration and anger More extensive history of cravings and other withdrawal symptoms More regular consumption of alcohol before treatment If a patient continues to drink excessively after many or ongoing procedures, their prognosis is very low. The effects of alcohol are often accompanied by chronic heavy drinkers.

By comparison to diabetes or congestive heart failure, drug use disorder is a chronic disease. When alcoholism is treated as a chronic disease, a success rate of 50% is close to that of other chronic diseases.

Chapter 3: Alcohol and its Impact

A bright color cosmopolitan is the drink of choice for glamorous characters in Sex and the City. James Bond is dependent on his famous martini to unwind after confounding a villain shaken, not stirred. And what marriage ends without a toast of champagne?

Alcohol is part of our society, relaxing and socializing, and our religious ceremonies are strengthened. But drinking too much on one occasion or over time can have serious health consequences. Many Americans agree that too much alcohol can lead to accidents and dependence. That's just part of the story, though. Alcohol abuse can destroy organs, weaken the immune system, and lead to cancers in addition to these serious problems. Plus, alcohol affects different people differently, much like smoking. Whether you develop an alcohol-related disease, genes, environment, and even diet can play a role. On the flip side, some people may actually profit from a small amount of drinking alcohol. Complicated sound? It can be certain. You need reliable, up-to-date information in order to stay healthy and to determine what role alcohol can play in your life. This brochure was intended to provide advice based on the latest findings on the effects of alcohol on your health.

Know the Amounts

Understanding how much alcohol a "normal" drink is can help you decide how much you drink and understand the risks. A typical drink contains around 0.6 ounces of liquid or 14 grams of pure alcohol. More familiarly, the following quantities represent one standard drink:

- 12 fluid ounces of beer (around 5 percentalcohol)
  - 8 to 9 malt liquor fluid ounces (about 7% alcohol)
- Five fluid ounces of table wine (around 12 percent alcohol)
- 1.5 fluid ounces of hard liquor (around 40 percent alcohol)

Research shows that men's consumption rates are no more than four drinks on' low-risk' For women, drinking rates of "low risk" on any given day are no more than three drinks AND no more than seven drinks a week. In order to remain low-risk, all single-day and weekly limits must be maintained.

Even within these guidelines, whether you drink too much, have health conditions, or are over 65 years of age, you may have problems. No more than three drinks should be available for older adults on any day and no more than seven drinks per week.

You may need to drink little or not at all on the basis of your health and how alcohol affects you. Those who should abstain from alcohol include those that:

- Consider driving a vehicle or operating machinery
- Are pregnant or attempting to become pregnant

- Take medications that interfere with alcohol

- Have a medical condition that can aggravate alcohol

3.1 Effects on the brain

You're talking with friends at a party, and a waitress comes around with champagne glasses. You're drinking one, then another, perhaps even a couple more. You laugh more loudly than usual before you realize it, and sway as you walk. You're too slow to move out of a waiter's way with a dessert tray by the end of the evening and have trouble talking clearly. When You wake up the next morning, feeling dizzy and hurting your brain. You can find it hard to recall all you've done the night before.

Such responses demonstrate how alcohol affects the brain rapidly and dramatically. The brain is a complex labyrinth of connections that keep our physical and psychological processes running smoothly. Disruption of any of these connections may affect the functioning of the brain. Alcohol can also have long-lasting effects on the brain, changing how it looks and works, resulting in a range of issues.

Most people don't realize how much alcohol can affect the brain. Yet knowing these potential consequences will help you make better choices about what amount of alcohol is right for you.

What happens inside the Brain?

The architecture of the brain is complex. It includes several systems that interact to support all the functions of your body, from thinking to breathing to moving.

By about a trillion small nerve cells called neurons, these multiple brain structures interact with each other. In the brain, neurons convert information into electrical and chemical signals that the brain can comprehend. They also send messages to the rest of the body from the brain.

Neurotransmitters are chemicals that carry signals between neurons. It can be very effective for neurotransmitters. Such chemicals can either enhance or decrease your body's reactions, emotions, and mood depending on the type and quantity of neurotransmitters. The brain only works to balance the neurotransmitters that accelerate things with those that slow things down to keep your body at the right place. Alcohol can slow the pace of neurotransmitter signaling in the brain.

Discovering the Brain Changes

We still do not understand how normally the brain works and how it is affected by alcohol. Scientists are constantly finding out how alcohol affects the mechanisms of brain interaction and alters the brain structure and the associated behavioral and functional consequences.

- Brain imaging Multiple imaging devices, including structural magnetic resonance imaging (MRI), functional magnetic resonance imaging (fMRI), To produce brain images, DTI, and positron emission tomography (PET) is used. MRI and DTI create images of the structure of the brain or the brain's appearance. FMRI investigates the role of the brain, or what the brain does. It can detect changes

  in the function of the brain. PET scans investigate changes in the role of the neurotransmitter. All these methods of imaging are useful for monitoring alcoholic brain changes. For example, to test potential relapses, they will demonstrate how an alcoholic brain changes immediately after stopping drinking, and again after a long period of sobriety.

- Researchers to assess how alcohol-related brain changes affect mental functioning also use psychological tests. These tests show how alcohol affects emotions and personality and how learning and memory skills are compromised.

- Clinical studies testing the effect of alcohol on animals ' brains help researchers better understand how alcohol affects the human brain and how abstinence can reverse this damage.

Defining the Brain Changes

Researchers identified the brain regions most vulnerable to alcohol effects using brain imaging and psychological testing. These include Cerebellum motor coordination is regulated by this region. Damage to the cerebellum results in loss of balance and stumbling, and cognitive functions such as memory and emotional response may also be affected.

- Limbic system This complex brain network controls a number of emotional functions. Damage affects each of these functions in this region.

- The cerebral cortex from this brain region will impair our ability to think, plan, behave intelligently and interact socially. This region also binds the brain to the rest of the nervous system. Changes and disruption to this environment are impairing the ability to solve, recall, and understand problems.

Alcohol Shrinks and Disturbs Brain Tissue

The delicate balance of neurotransmitters can be thrown off course by heavy alcohol intake, even on one occasion. Alcohol can cause the information to be transmitted too slowly by your neurotransmitters, so you feel extremely drowsy. Neurotransmitter balance alcohol-related disruptions can also trigger mood and behavioral changes, including depression, agitation, loss of memory, and even seizures.

Long-term, heavy drinking causes neuronal changes, such as cell size reductions. Because of these and other changes, the brain mass is diminishing, and the internal cavity of the brain is growing larger. These changes can affect a wide range of skills, including motor coordination, temperature control, Rest, mood, and different cognitive functions, like memory and learning. One particularly susceptible neurotransmitter to even small amounts of alcohol is called glutamate. Glutamate affects memory, among other things. Researchers believe that alcohol interferes with the activity of glutamate, and this may cause some people to "pass out" temporarily, or forget much of what happened during a heavy drinking night.

Alcohol also causes increased serotonin release, another neurotransmitter that helps regulate emotional expression, and endorphins, which are natural substances that can trigger relaxation and euphoria as intoxication sets in. Scientists now realize that these disturbances are being compensated by the brain. Despite the presence of alcohol, neurotransmitters adapt to create balance in the brain. But making these adjustments can have negative results, including building alcohol tolerance, developing alcohol dependence, and having symptoms of withdrawal from alcohol.

What Factors Make a Difference

Different reactions to alcohol are different. That's because there is a range of factors that can influence the reaction of your brain to alcohol.

- The more you drink, the more fragile your brain becomes, and how often you drink.
- Genetic background and family history of alcohol Some ethnic populations may have stronger alcohol reactions, and problem drinkers are more likely to develop genetic alcohol heritage and family history Certain ethnic populations may be more likely to respond to alcohol, and children of alcoholics are more likely to develop alcoholics.
- Physical health the effects of alcohol can take longer to wear off if you have liver or diet issues.

Are brain Problems Reversible

A lack of alcohol over a period of several months to a year may allow partial correction of structural brain changes. Abstinence can also help to reverse negative effects on the ability to think, including problem solving, memory, and attention.

Other Alcohol-related Brain Conditions

Liver damage affecting the brain Alcoholic liver disease not only affects the function of the liver itself but also damages the brain. The liver breaks down alcohol and the toxins that it releases. Alcohol by-products damage liver cells during this process. These things damaged liver cells no longer function as they should and enable too many of these toxic substances, particularly ammonia and manganese, to travel to the brain. Such drugs cause brain cell damage, leading to a serious catastrophic brain disorder called hepatic encephalopathy.

There are a number of problems with hepatic encephalopathy, ranging from less serious to fatal. These issues might include:

- Sleep disturbances
- Mood and personality change
- Anxiety
- Depression
- Shortened attention span
- Coordination problems, including asterixis, resulting in handshaking or flapping
- Coma
- Death

Doctors may help treat hepatic encephalopathy with compounds that reduce ammonia concentration in the blood. Patients with hepatic encephalopathy, in some cases, need a liver transplant, which usually helps boost brain function.

Fetal alcohol spectrum disorders-at any stage of development, alcohol can affect the brain even before birth. Disorders of the fetal alcohol spectrum are the full range of physiological, cognitive, and behavioral problems and other birth defects arising from exposure to prenatal alcohol. Fetal alcohol syndrome (FAS), the most serious of these disorders, is characterized by abnormal facial characteristics and is usually associated with a severe reduction in brain function and overall growth. FAS is the leading preventable birth defect in the United States today associated with mental and behavioral impairment. Children's brains with FAS are smaller than normal and have fewer cells, including neurons. These shortcomings lead to lifelong learning and behavioral problems. Current research is exploring whether the brain function of children and adults with FAS can be enhanced through comprehensive therapy education, dietary supplements, or medication

3.2 Effects on the Heart

Americans know how widespread heart disease is about 1 in 12 of American suffer from it. The links between heart disease and alcohol are not always obvious. For decades, on the one hand, scientists have known that excessive consumption of alcohol can damage the heart. Drinking so much for a long time or drinking too much on a single occasion can jeopardize your heart and life. On the other side, scientists now know that drinking small amounts of alcohol can protect certain people's hearts from the risks of coronary artery disease.

Decide how much alcohol is right, if any, because it can be difficult for you. You need to know the main facts and then consult your doctor to make the best decision for yourself.

Know the function:

Your heart, blood vessels, and blood make up the cardiovascular system. This system constantly works every second of your life to supply your cells with oxygen and nutrients, and to carry carbon dioxide and other unnecessary material.

This cycle is guided by your brain. It is a muscle that continues to contract and relax, pushing the blood along the path that is required. The heart pumps 100,000 times a day, pumping around the body the equivalent of 2,000 gallons of blood.

The two sides of the heart, or chambers, gather blood and pump it back into the body. The right heart ventricle pumps blood into the lungs to exchange oxygen from the cells with carbon dioxide. The heart calms to allow the left chamber to return to the blood. It then pumps into tissues and organs the oxygen-rich blood. The blood that passes through the kidneys helps the body to get rid of waste products. Electrical signals keep the heart continuously beating and Propelling this routine at the appropriate rate

Know the Risks

Alcoholic cardiomyopathy: long-term heavy drinking weakens the muscle of the heart, causing an alcoholic cardiomyopathy disorder. A tired heart sinks and expands and is unable to contract efficiently. As a consequence, it cannot pump enough blood to feed the organs properly. A lack of blood flow causes serious damage to organs and tissues in some cases. Cardiomyopathy signs include shortness of breath and other problems with breathing, exhaustion, swollen feet and legs, and irregular heartbeat. It can even result in brain damage.

Arrhythmias: Both drinking binge and long-term drinking can influence how quickly heartbeats. In order to keep this running at the right speed and continuously, the heart relies on an internal pacemaker system. Alcohol disrupts this pacemaker system, causing the heart to beat too quickly or irregularly. Such irregularities in the heart rate are called arrhythmias. Two types of alcoholinduced arrhythmias are: Arial fibrillation chambers shudder weakly but do not contract in this form of arrhythmia, the upper or atrial heart. Blood can accumulate and even clot in these upper chambers. If a blood clot passes from the heart to the brain, a stroke may occur; if it extends to other organs like the lungs, the blood vessel may be embolized or blocked.

This type of arrhythmia occurs in the ventricular tachycardia lower or ventricular chambers of the core. Electrical signals travel across the muscles of the heart, triggering contractions that keep blood flowing at the right place. Alcohol-induced damage to cells of the heart muscle can cause the electrical impulses to travel too many times through the ventricle, triggering too many contractions. The heart beats so hard, so, between each beat, it doesn't fill up with enough blood. Therefore, not enough blood is supplied to the rest of the body.

Ventricular tachycardia is responsible for dizziness, lightheadedness, unconsciousness, cardiac arrest, and even sudden death. Drinking to excess on a particular occasion may cause either of these anomalies, particularly when you don't usually drink. In these cases, the problem is called "winter heart syndrome," since people who usually don't drink at parties can consume too much alcohol during the holiday season. Excessive drinking, in the long run, changes the course of electrical impulses that regulate the heart's beating, causing arrhythmia.

Strokes: When blood cannot reach the brain, a stroke occurs. For about 80% of strokes, a blood clot prevents blood flow to the brain. These are known as ischemic strokes. Blood also builds up in the brain, or in the surrounding spaces. It triggers strokes that are hemorrhagic.

Even in people without coronary heart disease, binge drinking, and long-term heavy drinking can lead to strokes. Recent studies show that people who drink are around 56% more likely to suffer an ischemic stroke over ten years than people who never drink. Binge drinkers are also about 39 percent more likely than people who never binge drink to suffer any type of stroke.

Furthermore, alcohol exacerbates the conditions that often lead to strokes, including hypertension, arrhythmias, and cardiomyopathy.

Hypertension: Chronic alcohol use can cause high blood pressure, or hypertension, as well as binge drinking. The blood pressure is a function of your heart's pressure as it beats, and the pressure within the veins and arteries. As the heart pumps blood into them, healthy blood vessels spread out as elastic. When the blood vessels stiffen, hypertension increases, making them less elastic. Heavy alcohol consumption causes certain stress hormones to be released, which in turn, restricts blood vessels. This increases blood pressure. Furthermore, alcohol can affect the muscle function within the blood vessels, causing blood pressure to be limited and elevated.

Know the Benefits

Research suggests that healthy people who drink moderate amounts of alcohol can have a lower risk of developing coronary heart disease relative to nondrinkers. Moderate drinking for men on a given day is usually defined as no more than two drinks and one drink per day for women who are not pregnant or who are trying to conceive.

There are many factors that can support the accumulation of fat in the arteries, including diet, genetics, high blood pressure, and age, leading to heart disease. An excess of fat narrows the arteries of the coronary, the blood vessels that directly supply the heart with blood. Clogged arteries reduce blood supply to the muscle of the heart and facilitate the formation of blood clots. Both heart attacks and strokes can result from blood clots.

Drinking moderately can protect your heart against these conditions, according to recent studies. Moderate drinking helps to prevent and reduce arterial fat buildup. It can increase blood levels of HDL or "healthy" cholesterol, which ward off heart disease. It can help prevent heart attack and stroke by preventing the formation of blood clots and by dissolving developing blood clots. Drinking moderately can also help to control blood pressure levels.

Such advantages may not apply to individuals with existing medical conditions or who take other medications regularly. Studies often prevent people from starting to drink just for the sake of safety. Alternatively, you can use this research to help you start a conversation about the best path for you with your medical professional.

3.3 Effects on the Liver

One of the leading causes of disease and death in the United States is liver disease. Nearly 2 million Americans suffer from alcohol-induced liver disease. In general, people who drink excessively over many years are affected by liver disease.

While many of us know that excessive consumption of alcohol can lead to liver disease, we may not know why. Understanding the alcohol-liver connections can help you make smarter drinking decisions and take better control of your health.

Know the Function

The liver is working hard to maintain a healthy and productive body. It stores nutrients and heat. It produces proteins and enzymes that your body uses to fend off infection and function. It also rids off your body of hazardous substances, including alcohol.

The liver breaks down most of the alcohol a person consumes. Yet breaking down alcohol creates chemicals that are even more harmful than alcohol itself. These byproducts destroy the cells of the liver, encourage inflammation, and weaken the natural defenses of the body. Such problems will ultimately interrupt the metabolism of the body and hinder the functioning of other organs.

Even though the liver plays an important role in the detoxification of alcohol, it is particularly vulnerable to alcohol damage.

Know the Consequences

While heavy drinking can cause fat to develop in the liver for a few days at a time. This condition, known as steatosis, is the earliest stage of alcoholic liver disease and the most severe liver disorder caused by alcohol. The extra fat makes it harder for the liver to function and leaves it open to harmful infection, such as alcoholic hepatitis.

For some, there are no clear signs of alcoholic hepatitis. Alcoholic hepatitis, however, can cause fatigue, vomiting, loss of appetite, abdominal pain, and even mental confusion for others. As the severity of alcoholic hepatitis increases, the liver is dangerously enlarged, causing jaundice, excessive bleeding, and difficulty in coagulation.
Fibrosis, which causes the formation of scar tissue in the liver, is another liver disease associated with heavy drinking. Alcohol alters the chemicals needed to break down this scar tissue in the liver and remove it. Liver function is suffering as a result.

If you keep drinking, this excessive scar tissue builds up and creates a condition called cirrhosis, which is a slow worsening of the liver. Cirrhosis prohibits the liver from performing critical functions such as infection control, blood removal of harmful substances, and nutrient absorption.

A variety of complications may result as cirrhosis weakens liver function, including jaundice, insulin resistance, and type 2 diabetes, and even liver cancer.

Risk factors ranging from genetics and sex to alcohol availability, drinking social customs, and even diet can affect the individual susceptibility of a person to alcoholic liver disease. Statistics show that approximately one in five heavy drinkers will develop alcoholic hepatitis, and cirrhosis will develop one in four.

Know there's a bright side

The great news is that a number of changes in lifestyle will help to prevent alcoholic liver disease. The most critical change in lifestyle is alcohol abstinence. Cessation of drinking will help prevent further liver injury. Both lead to alcoholic liver disease through smoking cigarettes, obesity, and poor nutrition. To keep the liver disease in check, it is important to stop smoking and improve your eating habits. Nevertheless, when conditions such as cirrhosis become serious, the primary treatment choice may be a liver transplant.

3.4 Effects on the Pancreas

Every year, more than 200,000 Americans are sent to the hospital for acute pancreatitis. Heavy drinkers are also many of those who suffer from pancreatic issues. Habitual and heavy drinking affects the pancreas, and pancreatitis is commonly caused.

Know the Function

The pancreas plays a significant part in the digestion of food, making it fuel for the body to work. It pushes enzymes into the small intestine to digest carbohydrates, proteins, and fat. It also secretes glucagon and insulin, hormones that control the use of glucose, the body's key source of energy. Insulin and glucagon control the glucose levels, making all cells use fuel glucose. Insulin also helps to store extra glucose as glycogen or fat.

Alcohol destroys pancreatic cells when you drink and affects insulin-involving metabolic processes. This process leaves dangerous inflammations open to the pancreas.

Know the Risks

The alcohol-free pancreas sends enzymes to the small intestine to metabolize food. This process is jumbling with alcohol. Instead of delivering the enzymes to the small intestine, it allows the pancreas to secrete the digestive juices. These enzymes and acetaldehyde, a substance that is produced by metabolizing or breaking down the alcohol, are harmful to the pancreas. When you regularly consume alcohol over a long period of time, this ongoing process will cause inflammation and tissue and blood vessel swelling.

This inflammation is called pancreatitis, which prevents the proper functioning of the pancreas. Pancreatitis, or acute pancreatitis, happen as a sudden attack. The inflammation can become persistent as excessive drinking continues. This disorder is referred to as chronic pancreatitis. Pancreatitis is also a risk factor for pancreatic cancer growth.

A heavy drinker could not detect pancreatic damage build-up until an attack is caused by the problems.

An acute pancreatic attack causes symptom such as

- Abdominal pain that can radiate back
- Nausea and nausea

- Fever

- Fast heart rate

- Diarrhea

- Sweating

Recurrent pancreatitis triggers such symptoms as well as severe abdominal pain, significant reduction of pancreatic function and digestion, and issues with blood sugar. Chronic pancreatitis gradually kills the pancreas, leading to diabetes or even death.

While a single drinking binge will not immediately lead to pancreatitis, the risk of contracting the disease will increase if excessive drinking happens over time.

Such risks extend to all heavy drinkers, but pancreatitis is established by only about 5 percent of people with alcohol dependence. Many people are more susceptible to the disease than others, but scientists have not yet determined specifically that there is a significant role to play in environmental and genetic factors.

Treatment Helps but does not Cure

Alcohol abstinence can delay pancreatitis development and reduce painful symptoms. Also, a low-fat diet can help. Protecting against infections and getting supportive treatment is also critical. Treatment options can improve pancreatic function, including enzyme replacement therapy or insulin. The procedure is necessary in some cases to relieve pain, remove blockages, and reduce attacks. It is possible to manage the effects of alcoholic pancreatitis, but not easily reversed.

3.5 Cancer Risks

Genetics, environment, and lifestyle habits can all increase your cancer risk. We cannot do anything to change our genes, and often to change our environment, we can't do much. But a different story is aboutlifestyle habits.

One lifestyle habit of drinking too much alcohol will increase your risk of developing certain cancers. That doesn't mean anyone who drinks too much is going to develop cancer. But the more you drink, the greater the chances of developing those types of cancer, the more numerous studies suggest.

A group of Italian scientists, for example, reviewed more than 200 studies examining the impact of alcohol on cancer risk. The combined findings of these studies show clearly that the greater the risk of developing a number of cancers, the more you drink. The National Cancer Institute as a risk factor for the following cancer types:

- Mouth

- Esophagus

- Pharynx

- Larynx.

Drinking 5 or more drinks a day can also increase the risk of other cancers, including colon or rectum cancer.

In reality, abstract figures from the recent report from the World Cancer Research Fund show that women who drink five regular alcohol drinks every day have around two times the risk of developing colon or rectal cancer compared to women who do not drink at all.

Often, people who drink are more likely to smoke, and the combination greatly increases the risk. For some cancers, cigarettes alone are a known risk factor. Smoking and drinking together, however, intensifies each substance's cancer-causing effects. The overall effect poses a risk that is even greater.

The risk of cancer of the throat and mouth is particularly high because both alcohol and tobacco are in direct contact with these regions. Together, people who drink and smoke are 15 times more likely than not-drinkers and non-smokers to develop mouth and throat cancers. Moreover, recent studies estimate that alcohol and tobacco together are responsible for:

- 80 percent of men's throat and mouth cancer

- 65 percent of women's throat and mouth cancer

- 80 percent of women's esophageal squamous cell carcinoma, a type of esophagus cancer
- 25 to 30 percent of all cancers of the liver

Women and Cancer

The study found that alcohol increases the chances of women developing breast, stomach, throat, rectum, liver, and esophageal cancers. Researchers connected alcohol to approximately 13% of these cases of cancer.

The study also concluded that the risk of cancer increases regardless of how little or what type of alcohol a woman drinks. Even one drink a day can increase the risk, and with each additional drink, it continues to rise. Although men have not been included in this study, researchers believe that this threat is likely to be similar to men.

The report also attributes alcohol in about 11% of all cases of breast cancer. This suggests this about 27,000 of the 250,000 breast cancer cases diagnosed in the U.S. in 2008 may come from alcohol.

Know the Reasons

Scientists are trying to figure out exactly how and why alcohol can cause cancer. There are a number of possible explanations.

Another reason is that alcohol itself is not the primary cancer cause. We know that alcohol metabolization or degradation results in harmful toxins in the body. Acetylaldehyde is one of these toxins. Acetylaldehyde destroys the cells ' genetic material and makes them unable to repair the damage. It also causes cells to grow too fast, making genetic changes and mistakes ripe for conditions. Cancer in cells with defective genetic material can grow more easily.

However, recent animal studies have shown that they cause the body to produce additional quantities of a protein called VEGF as cells attempt to break down alcohol. VEGF stimulates blood vessel development and organ tissue growth. Too much VEGF on the flip side, though, is that it enables blood vessels to expand in cancer cells that die alone. It makes it possible for cancer cells to grow into tumors.

We also know that causing cirrhosis, alcohol will damage the liver. When too much scar tissue builds up inside the liver, cirrhosis occurs and leaves it unable to perform its vital functions. Liver cancer is one of the many complications that can be caused by cirrhosis.

Hormones can be the link between alcohol and cancer of the breast. Alcohol, including estrogen, can increase the amounts of certain hormones in the body. Excess estrogen can lead to cancer of the breast.

Eventually, some heavy drinkers can have genes that play a role in preventing the development of cancer. A European research team looked at 9,000 people with similar lifestyle habits to determine why some developed mouth and throat cancers, while others did not. Of the participants who were heavy drinkers, there was a particular genetic alteration among those who did not develop cancers that allowed them to break down alcohol about 100 times faster than those without. The study showed that this gene is the reason that in reaction to heavy drinking, certain people are less likely to develop cancer.

Know there's a Bright Side

Thankfully, studies show that by drinking less, you will reduce the cancer risk. A current Canadian report from 1966 to 2006 analyzed studies and concluded that risk reduction is possible, particularly for head and neck cancers. The study showed that their risk of developing cancer decreased when people abstained from drinking. Despite 20 years of abstinence, former smokers had the same risk of head and neck cancer as those who never drank.

Effects on the immune system

All around us are germs and bacteria. The immune system is, luckily, designed to protect the bodies from numerous foreign substances that can make us sick. Drinking alcohol weakens the immune system, making the fight against disease even harder for your organization. Understanding the effect of alcohol on your immune system can inform your decisions about alcohol consumption.

Know the Facts

Compared to an army, your immune system is often. This army is protecting the body against illness and infection.

The skin and mucous heritage of your respiratory and gastrointestinal tracts help block bacteria from entering your body or remaining in it. If foreign substances make it through these barriers somehow, your immune system with two defensive systems kicks into gear: innate and adaptive.

Before you are exposed to foreign substances such as bacteria, viruses, fungi, or parasites, the innate system exists in your body. These substances can invade your body and make you sick, which are called antigens. White blood cells from your first line of defense against infection. They quickly surround and swallow foreign bodies.

- Natural killer cells (NKs) Natural killer cells are different white blood cells that recognize and destroy cancer or virus-infected cells.

- Cytokines White blood cells transmit directly to a contaminated site these chemical messengers. Cytokines cause inflammatory reactions, such as blood vessels dilating and increasing blood flow to the affected area. More white blood cells are also called upon to swarm an infected area.

- After you are first exposed to an infection, the adaptive system kicks in. Your adaptive system fights it off faster and more efficiently than the first time the next time you encounter the same disease.

- T-lymphocyte cells T-cells improve the function of white blood cells by attacking specific foreign substances. A Big range of bacteria and viruses can be detected and killed by T-cells. Infected cells can also be destroyed, and cytokines secreted.

- B-lymphocyte cells B-cells produce antibodies to counter harmful substances by adhering to them and separating them from other immune cells.

- Antibodies They produce antibodies when B-cells encounter antigens. These are proteins that hit specific antigens and then recognize that they can be combated with antigen.

Know the Risks

Innate and adaptive immune systems are weakened by alcohol. Chronic alcohol use reduces white blood cells ' ability to swallow harmful bacteria effectively. Excessive drinking also disrupts cytokine production, causing either too much or not enough of these chemical messengers to be produced by your body. An abundance of cytokines can damage your tissue, while a shortage of cytokines will leave you open to infection.

Chronic alcohol use also suppresses T-cell growth and may hinder NK cells ' ability to attack tumor cells. This decreased activity leaves you more vulnerable to bacteria and viruses and less likely to kill cancer cells.

Chronic consumers are more likely than people who don't drink too much to develop diseases like pneumonia and tuberculosis with a compromised immune system. Evidence also connects the damage caused by alcohol to the immune system with increased vulnerability to HIV infection. For chronic drinkers who already have the disease, HIV progresses more rapidly.

You can also weaken the immune system by drinking a lot on a single occasion. Drinking to intoxication can slow the ability of your body to produce cytokines that prevent infection by causing inflammation. Without these inflammatory responses, the strength of your body to defend itself against bacteria is significantly reduced. A recent study shows that slower development of inflammatory cytokines will reduce the ability to fight off infections after drinking for up to 24 hours.

Still Looking for the Bright Side

At this point, scientists do not know if abstinence, decreased drinking, or other interventions can help to reverse the immune system effects of alcohol. Nonetheless, avoiding drinking helps minimize the strain on your immune system, particularly if you are battling a viral or bacterial infection.

3.6 Personality Factors

Many people are more likely than others to develop alcoholism. For example, people who are more likely to pursue or ignore the danger, such as those who are less inhibited, are more likely to engage in heavy drinking. Personality variables, like genes, are incredibly complicated and interact with each other. Someone who just wants to be "the party's life" may become a massive social drinker because they believe that when drunk.

They are more "like," and somebody with intense shyness may become a heavy drinker to alleviate their discomfort in social situations. The individual's perceptions of drinking also play a significant role. People with optimistic opinions about the impacts of alcohol are more likely to develop an addiction than people with negative expectations of the effects of alcohol.

Personal Choice Factors

In terms of addiction, there are certain forms of personal choice. For example, someone who has decided never to have a drink would certainly not develop alcoholism. However, those who choose to avoid social environments in which drinking is likely to occur are also less likely to develop an addiction. Nonetheless, once an individual start to drink personal choice, the effect on whether they become an alcoholic relative to other variables will be considerably less.

Drinking History Factors

The history of drinking affects a person's likelihood of developing addiction significantly. Those with a long tradition of drinking are more likely to become alcoholics than someone who has been drinking alcohol for less time. Likewise, people who have consumed more alcohol are more likely than people who have consumed less alcohol to become an alcoholic. In reality, alcohol use rewires the brain to crave and rely on alcohol, and these are cumulative effects.

Genetic Factors

Several studies have concluded that no single factor has as much effect as the genes of that person on whether or not someone becomes an alcoholic. Biological children of alcoholics, whether raised by alcoholics or nonalcoholics, are significantly more likely to become alcoholics. Likewise, alcoholic-educated non-biological children are less likely to become alcoholics than alcoholic-educated biological children.

Alcoholism's genetics are incredibly complicated and far from being fully understood. It is not a single gene that causes addiction, but a large number of genes that interact with each other. At least 51 genes were discovered that had an impact on alcoholism. Genetics has an impact on many alcohol aspects. Genetics, for instance, affect how easily and quickly addiction breaks down, how bad hangovers are, how much alcohol a person feels, how much an individual looks for risky behaviors, and how likely someone is to stop or continue to drink.

With the exception of genetics, the family life of an individual plays an important role in the likelihood of developing alcoholism. People who grow up in a family that practices or even promotes heavy drinking are more likely to develop alcoholism. Heavy drinking is standardized and glamorized in these families, making it socially acceptable, expected, and potentially desirable.

Environmental Factors

In alcoholism, somebody resides. The acquisition of alcohol is considerably harder and more expensive in some countries and states. With less exposure, a person is less likely to develop alcoholism. The more alcohol is present in a setting, the more likely a person is to develop alcoholism. The wealth of the family also plays a role. Individuals with higher family wealth are much more likely to consume alcohol and develop problems in the use of alcohol. In the U.S., 78 percent of people with an annual household income of $75,000 a year drink, while only 45 percent of people with an annual household income of less than $30,000 drink.

Religious Factors

While somebody of any faith may become an alcoholic, people who are strict adherents of religions that are strongly opposed to alcohol are less likely to become alcoholics. This is especially true when local laws, social practices, and alcohol availability are strongly influenced by religion. Islam, Mormonism, Evangelical Protestantism, and Orthodox Judaism are some of the most widely studied examples.

Social and Cultural Factors

Alcoholism is affected by many social and cultural factors. Alcohol abuse problems are generally more likely to occur where drinking is normal or promoted. Perhaps the most frequently cited example is college, where alcohol consumption is widely celebrated and accepted, including particularly hazardous types of drinks such as binge drinking.

Therapy is also affected by social and cultural factors. Societies, where drinking is deemed shameful, can lead alcoholics to conceal their addiction and seek treatment Because of the stigma of being known as an alcoholic. Drinking is influenced by both dominant and subcultures. Members of certain subcultures are more likely to engage in alcohol abuse, which is actively encouraged by other members in many cases and considered a form of acceptance.

Age Factors

The probability of abuse of alcohol is strongly influenced by the age of an individual. In late teens, alcohol use usually begins in the early twenties, peaks in the late twenties to mid-twenties, and slows down in the early thirties. People are most likely to abuse alcohol in the early to mid-twenties, suffering from substance use disorders. Nevertheless, the younger a person begins to drink alcohol, the more likely they are to develop alcoholism later in life. This relates especially to people beginning to drink before the age of 15.

Educational Factors

The more educated a person is, generally speaking, the more likely he or she is to drink alcohol. 80% of college graduates drink in the United States, while only 52% drink without college drinks. College graduates who drink are 61 percent more likely than non-college graduates who drink to say they've been drinking alcohol in the last 24 hours. For example, training often influences certain drinking habits. U.S. college graduates strongly prefer beer to wine, while non-college students prefer beer to wine.

Career Factors

Many occupations are more likely than others to develop alcoholism. This is particularly true with respect to high stress, high-risk professions, or those dominated by younger adults. Military members, in particular, are more likely to develop disorders of alcohol use. Employment usually affects the consumption of alcohol.

Known Specific Risk Factors

- Consumption of more than 15 drinks per week for men or 12 drinks per week for women

- Binge drinking (consumption of more than five or more drinks every 2 hours for men or four or more drinks per 2 hours for women)

- Biological family members with alcoholism or drug addiction

- Problems in mental health such as bipolar disorder, depression, or anxiety It is important to remember that there is no risk factor that determines the future, and the past does not dictate.

Treatment practitioners have many years of experience working with them all sorts of risk factors and drug addicts from all walks of life, and they know how to help you. Or locate a rehabilitation facility now, contact a committed care specialist to help you navigate through your past and present to get you into the future.

Chapter 4: How to Quit Drinking

Changing your behavior is just one aspect of reducing your dependence on alcohol, but it's significant, and there's a difference between quitting alcohol and avoiding alcohol.

Controlling pressure, decisions, and even your diet will eliminate barriers that keep you away from dependency on alcohol on a daily basis. Not everyone is experiencing the same withdrawal of alcohol. In fact, there are things you can do to move it along quickly.

For some men, it's just that to kick back with a glass or two of wine. You're going out with mates. You're pouring, and you're sipping, you have that hot, relaxed feeling. One glass becomes many for many, one night out becomes every night, and alcohol begins to take on a wide mental space that becomes the focus of your life. One glass becomes many for many, one night out becomes every night, and alcohol begins to take on a wide mental space that becomes the focus of your life.

4.1 How Alcohol Addiction Works

If you are addicted to something, that does not mean that you are weak or unwilling. Addiction lives in the circuitry of your brain; it's not a personal weakness.

In your brain, addictive substances such as alcohol cause receptors for pleasure. The more frequently you turn on your paths of pleasure, the less pleasure you feel over time. And, to get those happy chemicals, the brain will be looking for stronger and stronger triggers. After so much repetition, your brain becomes accustomed to the stimulus, and over time you're so used to it that you've got to have your fix to work.

4.2 Quit
Drinking Good
Habits

No matter you are starting a new habit or breaking an old habit, success depends on three things:

- Changing your behavior either starting a new behavior or stopping one

- Willpower being physically and mentally resilient to moments of weakness and temptation

- Often you have to change your way of seeing yourself in the world. Essentially, stopping alcohol has three distinct phases:

- Detox get all the nasty things that have been built up from years of drinking from your body

Begin the path to comprehensive recovery by understanding that you need all these variables to work together; you can put around each other your plan to drop the bottle.

Willpower

You have a range of experiences as you hear stories about how people stop drinking. Many alcoholics simply decide that they want to try and stop drinking and never look back. Others go through a series of stops and relapses until they decide to check into a residential rehabilitation center.

Alcoholism is not merely a matter of willing power. Executive Director of the National Association for Providers of Addiction Treatment says, "The mechanisms of brain selection during addiction are actually damaged. Although behavioral disorders require an aspect of control and choice and practice, it would be incorrect not to understand that addiction is a brain disease, and the mechanisms of choice of the frontal lobes are actually broken. You possibly couldn't help yourself when you thought you couldn't help yourself in a situation.

Chances of Success

When you stop drinking, both of you have to change your environment in order to remove the temptation and be resilient when the temptation hits.

The explanation for this is that you have different levels of reasoning involved in making decisions. Speak of highlevel thinking as the human brain that is more advanced. You can think things through when you're relaxed, weigh pros and cons, predict results in your mind, and make the best decision possible.

High-level reasoning helps you to pause and consider rationally that it's not worth it until you take that first sip of alcohol.

Speak of thought at the lower level as the internal brain of the Labrador. You're more impulsive when you let your Labrador think for you Labradors chase moving cars and eat roadkill without a shred of thinking about what's going on after that. When your survival instincts kick in, you shift to this lower level of thinking when you feel hungry, stressed, or afraid. This is because the brain of the Labrador makes decisions based on the reward system of your brain.

You see a frosty mug of beer when you use lower-level thinking, and your brain says, "Go get that." And you do.

Alcohol makes the reward system for your brain think you need it to survive. You should analyze this thoroughly and consider the consequences if you do everything you can to keep the human brain working. You will be able to turn off those alcohol-seeking habits by keeping the Labrador brain quiet's

A Diet Can Help

It may seem difficult to think about changing the way you eat at the same time as you try to stop drinking. Stable blood sugar, however, helps you make better decisions throughout the day. When your sugar level in blood drops and you feel hungry, the brain of the Labrador begins to bark for food and anything else that goes into their field of vision. Cutting sugar and starchy foods avoid bursts of energy, leading to cranky, impulsive behavior. It depends instead on high-quality fats that will keep you full for longer.

Reduce the Number of Decisions

All the little choices you make during the day add up. Why? Just like your body, your mind gets tired. Before you need to replenish your cognitive resources, you have a small number of decisions you can make at any time. That's why at the end of a long day, willpower is weakest.

- Automate expenses, so you don't have to stress about them

- Meal prep lunches for the week so you don't know what to pack every morning

- Prepare clothes for the week or use a capsule wardrobe so you can dress up without thinking

- Make a routine with your workout buddy, so you don't have to worry about it. It's really nice to be free of decision-making fatigue when dealing with important ones like taking the drink or not.

Practice Mindfulness

You can measure your desire to act before you actually act when you pay attention to what you are doing. This holds the human brain in balance, and the brain of the Labrador silent.

Not only does it boost your consciousness for a few minutes of daily meditation, but it also enhances the prefrontal cortex of your brain. This is significant because of researchers associate deficiencies in the pre-frontal cortex with addiction. Meditation is one of the interesting ways to increase your resilience that you can do anywhere, without the necessary equipment.

Manage Stress

It's not that easy to resist impulses when you're stressed out. One study showed that alcohol exposure had no effect on the desire for alcohol when it was relaxed. When people were more stressed or in a bad mood, the participants in the alcohol-dependent study wanted a drink. To minimize stress, you can try Meditation Yoga Breathing techniques. Keeping down your stress will also keep your Labrador brain calm. This makes it easier to hold out of your mouth the glass of wine.

4.3 Withdrawal and Detoxing

Once you stop drinking, you can experience a variety of withdrawal symptoms such as

- Anxiety
- Mood disorders
- Sleep disturbances
- Shakiness, twitchiness
- Uneasiness or impending doom
- Depression

- Sweating

- Confusion

- Hallucinations (heavy drinkers)

The severity of your withdrawal symptoms and how long they last. They usually start eight hours after your last drink and peak after 24 to 72 hours, though if you were a very heavy drinker, symptoms might last for a few weeks.

Withdrawal of alcohol can range from significantly uncomfortable to serious and life-threatening, depending on how much your body has adapted to the effects of alcohol. Lighter regular drinkers may just need some aspects of it to power. In a medically controlled setting, heavy drinkers should detoxify. Sometimes it's hard, to be honest about how much you've been drinking with yourself, so letting a professional make this call is probably wise. Involve the procedure with your doctor.

You can do any things that help move along with the milder aspects of withdrawal from alcohol. Here are some awesome ways to make the process of withdrawal simpler and to get through the detox as quickly as possible.

Consider Glutathione

Once you detox from alcohol, you want to get the substances that make it as difficult as possible to get out of your system. Your body produces a potent antioxidant, glutathione, in the liver that helps detoxify your body. If you have all the building blocks in your body, your liver will have the best chance to make the right amount of glutathione to help you with it. 2 to 4 tablespoons of whey protein have all the precursors on a deck that you need to produce it.

Activated Charcoal

Toxic substances and heavy metals (including alcohol) are charged positively, and charcoal binds to positively charged ions and helps the body absorb them. Alcohol contains yeast that leaves tons of chemicals such as aldehydes and ammonia in your body when it dies off. Upon long-term drinking of yeast by-products and impurities from the production process, there is a lot of cleaning to do. Toxic substances and heavy metals (including alcohol) are charged positively, and charcoal binds to positively charged ions and helps eliminate them from your body. In reality, doctors in emergency rooms prescribe charcoal on a regular basis to treat overdoses. You should take charcoal in order to help you through the detox cycle. It is also bound nutrients from the food you eat, so just take them if you need them.

The charcoal will bind the active ingredients in prescriptions, so a quick chat with your pharmacist can help you do the right thing if you are taking medication. A good way to choose a charcoal capsule that's made from fine-ground coconuts in the United States, rather than from cow bones who knows where.

Quitting Alcohol vs. Avoiding Alcohol

Most alcoholics find that it does not work to reduce alcohol or wean it down, particularly during early recovery. To prevent relapses, they have to quit alcohol completely.

It's one thing to quit alcohol. The beast is to avoid alcohol. The temptation must be avoided because alcoholics have a different physical and emotional reaction than normal drinkers do when faced with an alcoholic beverage or other drinking indications.

Keep Alcohol out of your House

The most I thing you can do to avoid alcohol is to get it out of your house. If you live alone, pouring it down the drain is easy enough and not running to the store's booze aisle when you make the decision.

However, if you have family members who drink and don't want to take it out of the home, it may be time to look at a new situation.

 The doctor points out, "In early recovery, if you're in the same setting you've been, it's very hard to stay in rehabilitation. That's why a residential treatment period is a very good idea because you're away from a very toxic atmosphere. "Family situations can be just as much an obstacle as situations with friends and roommates.

"The families are not expected to be safe. Family systems are often very ill, and alcoholism is a disease of the family. It is often passed on. It's not a good place to come back if your home is sick, " Doctor says.

"There's really no problem for people who have been sober for a long time. They're going to a party, going to a vacation event, even going to a bar. It's all right. But not in early recovery. You've got to have security. Sober living is advised after initial intensive treatment. Live with other similarly positioned people who are trying for a period of time to maintain a healthy lifestyle. We find it to be step-down treatment.

"And perhaps you're not going back to the original world. It depends on how sick it has been. "Some people must forever avoid tempting situations. Others are never looking back. Be mindful of your habits, and be honest about what you can do about yourself.

For example, if you want to go fishing and that usually means drinking all day, you might need to stop fishing for a while. Some people may need a completely new hobby to replace fishing. If you and your buddies are brunching with mimosas on Sunday, there's not enough time to miss the mimosas during early recovery. You may need to miss all of the brunches.

Arrange parties at the epicenter with something else to preserve your social life. Go kayaking, hiking, playing board games, do it with friends whatever you love doing.

Lifestyle

Success depends on having peer support in place after an intensive period. Alcoholics Anonymous is a highly spiritual organization that focuses on the idea that you will be guided by a higher power through difficult times. This is great news if you have a practice of religion in place some practice at all because it is a non-specific god.

If you're not referring to the notion of a higher power, that's perfectly fine. Programs such as SMART Recovery use many of the same principles to provide a secular approach. The doctor suggests that services such as equine therapy and Phoenix Multi-sport offer peer support while helping people relate in new ways to the environment.

It is Never "kicked."

The doctor points out that alcoholism is never entirely past you. There's always the possibility of relapse. Rather than thinking about it as something you have done that you can un-do, imagine a path, a dedication to a new way of life, to healing. Know that ways to get to the other side are available. When alcohol no longer holds you, your days will be happier, safer, and satisfying.

Quitting alcohol it's not easy, and it will be the toughest during the first few days. You will do whatever it takes to be free from alcohol dependence, and it will take you a long way to believe that you are going to do it.

Chapter 5: Overcoming Alcohol Addiction

Are you prepared to stop drinking or cut to a higher level? These methods can help you get off the road to recovery.

It can be a long and bumpy road to overcome alcohol addiction. It may even seem impossible at times. But this is not the case. If you're willing to stop drinking and get the support you need, you will heal from the abuse of alcohol, no matter how heavy the drink is or how weak you feel. But you don't have to stay until you reach the rock's bottom; you can adjust it at any time. Those tips will help you get started on the road to recovery today, whether you want to stop drinking entirely or cut to safer rates.

Most people with alcohol problems do not choose to change their drinking habits immediately or make a big change out of the blue. Generally, recovery is a more gradual process. Denial is a huge obstacle in the early stages of transition. You will make excuses and drag your feet even after admitting that you have a drinking problem. Recognizing your ambivalence about stopping drinking is critical. If you're not sure if you're willing to change or struggling with the decision, it can help you think about each choice's costs and benefits.

5.1 Evaluating the Costs

Create a table such as those below that compares drinking benefits and costs against the benefits and costs of stopping.

Is Drinking Worth

It helps me to forget my problems.

- When I drink, I'm having fun.

- After a stressful day, it is my way to relax and unwind.

Benefits of not Drinking

- My friendships are likely to improve.

- Mentally and physically, I should feelbetter.

- For the people and things, I care about, I would have more time and energy.

Costs of Drinking

- It has caused my relationship problems.

- I'm sad, nervous, and surprised.

- My job performance and family obligations were messed with.

Costs of not Drinking

- I would need to find a different way to handle problems.

- I'd miss my friends drinking.

- I'd have to face the responsibilities that I didn't know.

Set goals and change strategies. The next move is to set clear drinking targets once the decision to change has been made.

The more precise the requirements are, the easier and more realistic, the better.

Residential Treatment

After three years, I cut back more than three drinks a day, three beers a weekend. Would you like to stop drinking or cut down on cutback? If your intention is to reduce your alcohol consumption, determine the days you're going to drink alcohol and how many drinks you're going to enjoy each day. Consider eating at least twice a week if you're not going to eat at all.

When would you like to stop drinking or drink less tomorrow? About the time of one week? The next month? Are you six months away? Set a specific quit date if you're trying to stop drinking.

Accomplish your Goals

Write down any suggestions on how to help you achieve those goals after you set your goals to either quit or cut back on your drinking. For example, for example:

Get rid of Temptations

Remove from your home and office all alcohol, barware, and other paraphernalia related to alcohol.

Announce your Goal

Let friends, family, and colleagues know you're trying to stop drinking or cut back on drinking. When they drink, remind them not to do so in front of you to help your recovery.

Stay up to date with your new limits. Make it clear that you will not be allowed to drink at home, and you may not be able to attend alcohol-serving activities.

Avoid bad Influences

Distance from people who do not support your efforts to stop drinking or to follow the boundaries that you have set. This could mean giving up any friends and social connections.

Learn from the Past

Focus on previous attempts to stop the drinking or growing it. What was going on? What wasn't that? What can you do to prevent mistakes this time differently?

Cutting Back vs. Quitting alcohol

Whether or not you would successfully reduce your problem with drinking depends on the extent of your drink problem. If you are an alcoholic saying, by definition, you are unable to regulate your drinking, and it is better to try to stop smoking altogether. If you're not prepared to take the step, and if you don't have an alcohol addiction issue but want to minimize it for private or ethical reasons, the below tips can help:

Set your Drinking Goal

Choose a limit on how much you're going to drink, but make sure that your target isn't more than one drink a day if you're a woman, two drinks a day if you're a male, and if you're a guy, you want a few days a week. Write down your target and keep it where you often see it, like on your phone or in the refrigerator. To help you reach your goal, keep track of your drink. Wrote down for Three to 4 months each time you get a drink and what you drink. You may be shocked when you discuss the results of your regular habits.

Cut down Drinking at home

Try to limit or remove your home alcohol. If you don't keep temptations around, it's much easier to avoid drinking.

Drink it more slowly. Drink slowly and have a 30-minute break or an hour break between drinks. And consume alcoholic beverages of soda, wine, and tea. Drinking on an empty belly is never a good idea, so before you drink, make sure to eat food.

Schedule one or two Days of Alcohol-Free Weekly Then try to stop one week of drinking. Take note about how you feel about these days physically and mentally recognizing the rewards will help you cut back for good.

Alcohol Addiction Treatment Options

Many people may stop drinking alone or with the aid of a 12-stage program or another support group, while others may require medical supervision to safely and comfortably detox from the drug. What is the best option for you depends on how much you have been drinking, how long you have had a problem, the stability of your living situation, and other health problems you may have?

Residential Treatment

Entails staying in a treatment facility while undergoing comprehensive daytime rehabilitation. This normally takes 30-90 days for residential treatment.

Partial Hospitalization

Is for persons requiring ongoing medical supervision but living in a stable situation. Generally, these treatment programs operate 3-5 days a week at the facility, 4-6 hours a day.

Intensive Outpatient Programs (IOP)

Focus on the prevention of relapse and can often be organized around the workplace or university.

Therapy (Individual, Group, or Family)

Support you in identifying the underlying causes of alcohol use, repair friendships, and learn how to manage healthy skills.

5.2 Finding the Best Treatment

No magic bullet or single treatment works for everyone. The needs of everyone are different, so finding a program that feels right to you is crucial. Any treatment program for alcohol addiction should be adapted toyour unique problems and circumstance.

It is not appropriate to limit care to doctors and psychologists. Some priests, social workers, and psychologists are also providing services for addiction treatment.

Treatment should go beyond even the abuse of alcohol. Addiction impacts your entire life, including your friendships, employment, education, and well-being.

The effectiveness in recovery relies on understanding how alcohol abuse has influenced you and developing a new lifestyle.

Commitment and follow-up are important. Recovery from alcohol addiction or heavy drinking is not a quick and easy process. Generally speaking, the more and more intense you use alcohol, the longer and more intense you will need the medication. Yet irrespective of the duration of weeks or months of the treatment program, long-term follow-up care is vital to your recovery.

Provide treatment for other issues in physical or mental health. Individuals often use alcohol to alleviate the symptoms of an undiagnosed condition of mental health, such as depression or anxiety.

It is also necessary to get care for any other psychological problems you are having when you seek help for alcohol addiction. Your best chance of recovery is to have the same care provider or group incorporate mental health and addiction treatment.

Withdrawing from Alcohol Safely

The body is physically dependent on alcohol if you drink heavily and frequently and withdraws if you stop drinking suddenly. Symptoms of alcohol withdrawal vary from mild to severe and include: P 6 Migraine trembling nausea or vomiting Stomach cramps and diarrhea Alcohol withdrawal symptoms usually occur within hours of withdrawal., peak in one day or two, and improve within five days. Yet withdrawal is not only painful in some alcoholics. It can be life-threatening. You may need medically supervised detoxification if you are a longterm, heavy drinker.

A detox may be done outpatient or in a hospital or alcohol treatment center where medicine may be administered to avoid medical complications and alleviate symptoms of withdrawal. Talk to your doctor or specialist for more details.

When you have any of the following signs of withdrawal, seek emergency medical attention: intense nausea confusion and disorientation fever hallucinations extreme episodes of agitation or seizures p 7 The above indications can be a sign of a severe form of alcohol withdrawal called delirium tremens or DTs. This unusual, emergency condition causes dangerous changes in how your brain controls your circulation and breathing, so getting to the hospital immediately is critical.

Get Support

Whether you choose to tackle alcohol addiction through rehabilitation, therapy, or a self-directed approach to treatment, support is essential. Try not to go it alone.

When you have friends, you can rely on for support, comfort, and guidance, it is much easier to heal from drug abuse or violence.

Support may come from family members, friends, counselors, other alcoholics who recover, your health care providers, and people from your community of faith.

Lean on close friends and family. It is an invaluable asset in rehabilitation to have the support of friends and family members. If you are hesitant to turn to your loved ones because you have already let them down, consider going to counseling for couples or family therapy.

Create a sober social network You may need to make some new connections if your previous social life revolved around alcohol. Having sober friends that will support your recovery is important. Try to take a class, join a church or group of citizens, volunteer, or attend community events.

Consider meetings a priority, joins a support group for rehabilitation, and regularly attend meetings.

It can be very helpful to spend time with people who understand exactly what you are going through. You may also learn from the common experiences of team members to learn what has already been learned to stay clean.

Find new Meaning in Life

It's just the start of your recovery from alcohol or heavy drinking while becoming sober is an important first step. Rehab or clinical care will get you on the road to recovery, but you will need to build a new, meaningful life where there is no place to drink in order to stay alcohol-free for the long term.

Five steps to a Sober Lifestyle

Pay attention to yourself. Eat fatty foods well and having more than enough rest to prevent changes in mood and hunger. Exercise is also essential: it releases endorphins, relieves stress, and fosters emotional well- being.

Build your network of supports. Surround yourself with positive influences and individuals that make you feel good about yourself. The more you invest in others and your community, the more you lose, which will help you stay motivated and on the path of recovery.

Develop new interests and activities. Find new interests, sports, or volunteer work, which will give you a sense of meaning and purpose. If you do stuff that you find enjoyable and drinking, you'll feel much better for yourself.

Achieve recovery If you are part of a support group such as Alcoholics Anonymous, have a sponsor, or are interested in counseling or an alcohol treatment program, the chances of remaining sober improve.

Discuss pressure in a healthy way. Misuse of alcohol is a mistaken attempt to deal with pressure. Find safe ways to keep the stress level under control, such as deep breathing, meditation, or other breathing exercises.

Plan for Triggers and Cravings

Alcohol cravings may be intense, especially during the first six years after you start drinking. Nice alcohol therapy prepares you for such challenges and helps you create new coping mechanisms to cope with stressful conditions, liquor cravings, and binge drinking pressure.

Avoiding Drinking Triggers

Stop the things that make you want to drink. If some men, locations, or behaviors cause an alcohol addiction to try to avoid them. This can mean major changes in your social life, how to find new stuff to do about your old childhood friends or leave those people and find a good one.

Throughout social settings, learn to say "no" to liquor. No of how much alcohol you're trying to avoid, you'll probably be offered a drink at times. Prepare ahead for how you'll react, with a firm, but respectful, "no thanks." **Managing Alcohol Cravings**

If you 're dealing with alcohol cravings, consider these strategies: Speak to someone you trust: your mentor, a supportive family member or friend, or someone from your faith community.

Distract until the desire is over. Go on a stroll, listen to music, do some home cleaning, go on an errand, or do a quick job.

Consider your excuses not to drink. There's a tendency to consider the positive effects of drinking when you want alcohol and forget the negative ones. Remember the long-term adverse effects of heavy drinking and how it doesn't make you feel better, even in the short term.

Consider the temptation and ride it out, rather than battling it. This is known as "urge surfing." Think of your appetite as an ocean wave that will soon be cresting, fracturing, and dissipating.

If you ride the urge out, without attempting to fight, judge, or disregard it, you will see that it moves quicker than you would expect.

The Three Basic Steps of Urge Surfing

Evaluate how you feel the craving. Sit in a comfortable chair on the floor with your feet flat and relaxed posture with your arms, take a few deep breaths, and focus on the inside. Wander through your body with your attention. Remember the part of your body where the desire is felt and what the feelings are like. Say to yourself how it feels. "My desire is in my mouth and nose and in my stomach, for example."

Focus on one area where you feel the urge. How do the emotions in this field look? Perhaps you feel warm, cold, tingly, or numb, for instance? Are your muscles relaxed or tense? How large is a region involved? Describe the feelings and any changes that may occur. "I feel dry and parched in my mouth. In my lips and tongue, there is pressure. I'm just drinking. I can imagine the smell and tingling of a drink as I exhale.

Repeat the desire on every part of your body. Which changes are taking place in the sensations? Notice how the urge is coming and going. You'll probably notice that the craving has disappeared after a few minutes. Urge surfing is not aimed at making cravings vanish, but at feeling them in a new way. Nonetheless, you can learn how to ride your cravings out with training, p 10 before they inevitably go down.

5.3 Handling Setbacks in your Recovery

Drug addiction is a method that often includes setbacks. Don't give up when you fall or relapse. A relapse drinking doesn't mean you're a loser, or you're not going to be able to achieve your goal. -relapse from drinking is an opportunity to learn and commit to sobriety, so in the future, you will be less likely to relapse.

If you fall, what to do: get rid of alcohol and get away from your break Note that one drink or a brief lapse doesn't have to turn into a full-blown relapse Don't let your feelings of guilt or shame deter you from getting back on track Call your therapist, counselor or a supportive friend for help

How to help Someone Stop Drinking

How to help someone avoid alcohol abuse and addictions It can be as heartbreakingly upsetting as frustrating to watch a family member suffer from a drinking problem. But while you are unable to do the hard work of overcoming your loved one's addiction. During their longterm rehabilitation, your love and support will play a crucial role.

Speak about your drinking to the guy. Share your thoughts in a compassionate way and seek support from your friend or family member. Try to remain impartial without debating, reading, blaming, or attacking.

Learn about addiction as much as you can. Study the types of treatment available and speak to your friend or family member about these choices.

Take action. Consider setting up a family meeting or intervention, but don't put yourself in a position of risk. Offer your help every step of the road to recovery.

Don't apologize for the actions of your loved one. The person with the issue of drinking must take responsibility for their actions. To shield somebody from the effects of drinking, don't lie or cover up things.

Don't be responsible for yourself. You are not to blame for the drinking problem of your loved one, and you cannot improve them.

Pay attention to yourself. On your own, you don't have to face it. Switch to trusted colleagues, a support group, or to help you deal with your own counselor. Not to ignore your own needs is also significant. Allow time to relax and do things that you enjoy.

5.4 How to Stop Drinking

Make a Commitment

(AA)Anonymous Alcoholics is an international mutual support group designed to enable its members to remain sober and to help other alcoholics accomplish sobriety.

To stop drinking without AA, you must make a serious commitment to yourself and those around you to change your drinking habits. Most people who have alcohol issues are denying how much they drink and how much it affects their lives. Even those who understand their drinking's consequences still tend to drag their feet and make excuses instead of initiating the drinking cycle. You have to get out of this mentality and commit yourself firmly to start the process, and you should make it public. Make a list of your drinking costs and benefits, as well as those you will reap if you don't drink. Eventually, let your family and friends know you've decided to limit or avoid your alcohol consumption, so they can support you by giving you positive reinforcement and reducing your exposure to alcohol and other causes when you're together.

Set Realistic Goals

Once you've decided to stop drinking, it's time to set your target. Many people may choose to stop drinking entirely, while others may choose to decrease the amount they drink or the number of times they engage in drinking. Set realistic goals so that you have the best chance of success for yourself. Follow the leadership of corporate America by selecting SMART-specific, measurable, agreed, realistic, and time-based goals. If you decide to stop drinking altogether, set the date on which you plan to start and at what point you think your goal will be achieved. If you just want to drink less, set up a specific plan to deal with that. You may decide that your target on any given day is not to drink more than two drinks, or you may decide to stop drinking just on weekdays. Whatever you want to do, let your friends and loved ones know that your plan is, so you've got the best opportunity to succeed.

Avoid all temptations

If you agree never to leave your house, you will eventually be put in alcohol-serving circumstances. Attempting to stick to your commitment in these circumstances can be difficult, especially for those who have committed to stop drinking without rehab or help from AA. Restrict or stop situations in which you may be tempted to indulge in alcoholic beverages, at least in the early stages of living up to your target, and attempting to improve your drinking habits. Instead of hitting the club circuit with friends for a happy hour, plan a home movie night or host the dinner party of a friend where you can control what is being served and how much. Do not socialize with friends and family members who drink too much alcohol, as this will put you right on the temptation track. If you're just trying to reduce your alcohol consumption, limit the amount of time you're staying at alcohol-serving functions or venues.

Learn to Cope with Cravings

Very certainly, as you go through the process of avoiding or reducing your alcohol intake, you will have to learn to cope with cravings and temptations. You may just want a beer, and maybe you don't even know why it's happening. You must learn to cope with these inner cravings as well as resisting temptations. Start by remembering why you've chosen to make a change and how far you've already come. Find someone you trust, whether you're a friend, doctor, or member of your family, and talk to them through the feelings. Learn to distract yourself by taking part in healthy alternatives such as going to the gym, meditating, engaging in sports, or just walking.

Understand the Alcohol Addiction Facts

Although it is readily available in most situations, alcohol is one of the most dangerous substances when it is not used properly. Because having too much alcohol impairs judgment significantly, people who have had too much to drink are often involved in reckless activities such as unprotected sex, violence, driving while intoxicated, and other behaviors that endanger themselves or others. Unfortunately, many people don't know about the facts of alcohol addiction and don't realize that the abuse of alcohol leads to long-term problems if it continues for a while. Severe conditions such as throat and liver cancer, liver disease, dementia, and cardiovascular disease are the consequences of alcohol abuse. Read about alcohol addiction information as much as you can to ensure that you are properly prepared for the process of alcohol detoxification. To stop drinking successfully, the first thing you need to do is to admit you have a problem that could have some serious consequences.

Check with your Doctor

Before beginning the alcohol detoxification process, make an appointment with your primary care doctor to review tips for stopping drinking, and whether or not you are well enough to stop drinking. In some cases, people with health issues are advised to wait until they are better to stop drinking. Typically, detoxification of alcohol only causes uncomfortable symptoms, but in rare circumstances, some of these symptoms may be dangerous. If you're in good enough health to stop drinking, your doctor can tell you. Trying to stop drinking at home without your primary care physician's approval is not advisable.

Ask your Doctor about Medicines

Some drugs will make a major difference in your healing journey by promoting the cycle of alcohol detoxification. One alcohol detoxification drug is disulfiram, which forces you to stop drinking when you consume alcohol by causing uncomfortable physical reactions. One drug to detoxify alcohol is acamprosate, a drug that helps to detoxify alcohol by increasing the symptoms of withdrawal and make the process of detoxification as comfortable as possible. If none of these alcohol detoxification drugs sound like they would help you stop drinking, consider asking your doctor about naltrexone, which simply blocks the ability of your brain to enjoy the highs that may result from alcohol consumption. Speak to your doctor about alcohol addiction and see if these drugs will help you stop drinking.

Join a Support Group

Join a Support Group in your community is a great way to build relationships with others who know exactly what you're doing. One reason that stopping drinking is difficult is that drinking is a social activity. When you're surrounded by drinking men, the temptation to enter them can be difficult to resist. If you're removed from a team, you'll make new friends who won't pressure you to compromise your goal soberly. It doesn't mean you've got to stop working with your old friends, but it allows you to realize that once you stop drinking, you have other social choices. However, if they can't understand why you want to stop drinking, you may have no choice but to distance yourself from some of your old friends. If people decide to stop drinking in some situations, their peers think their newly sober buddies think they're better than everyone else. It leads to anger and a willingness to break the promise to stop drinking.

Enroll in a 12-step Program

Structured 12-step programs arc vcry useful recovery tools. They also offer a wealth of facts about alcohol addiction. For some who have been dealing with alcohol addiction, 12 Step programs were the only things that helped them to stop drinking. One classic organization using a 12-step program is Alcoholics Anonymous, an association in a support-group form that has a program in almost every community. 12 Step programs are set of specific guidelines or spiritual principles outlining recovery plans for addicted people, regardless of what addiction might be. In regular support groups, however, most of the 12 step programs rely on some degree of anonymity to ensure that no one feels that opening up to the other participants would not be safe. If you are trying to find a way to meet new people, be sure to visit a regular support group as well.

Stay at an Alcohol Detox Center

Though living at a detox center is either impractical or difficult for many people, Detox facilities make a difference for free-to-visit patients. Even if you have a prescription like acamprosate, avoiding drinking at home may be painful. Nonetheless, you have access to a variety of effective medications at a detox center that will ease your symptoms and make stopping drinking easier. Employees at quality detox centers are compassionate, professional, and used to dealing with even the worst symptoms of withdrawal when they first stop drinking. Since stopping drinking is potentially dangerous if your body is dependent on alcohol, one of the best ways you can detox is to go through the detox phase under the guidance of trained medical professionals. Worst of all, you don't have a chance to relax in the midst of the detoxification cycle when you go to a detox center. You should rest assured that if you go to a detox center, you will go back soberly. The Refuge in Ocklawaha, Florida, is one example of a reputable detox center. The Refuge is a healing center based on the 12-step program for people suffering from any type of trauma, including PTSD, sexual abuse, physical abuse that may lead to addictions to substances.

Tell Everyone

Let everybody know what you're doing from your spouse to your children to your boss. The more people you know, the more people you will help. You cannot be shot for alcoholism, by the way. You may need to be temporarily reassigned if you are in a high-risk job until you can prove your sobriety, but you are legally protected. Alcoholics in your life are the only ones who will see, leaving alcohol as a bad thing. They're just too afraid or frail to do what you're doing.

Find New Things to Do

If your life has been about alcohol, you'll need new things. Seek to go to a bowling alley or driving range if you used to sit at a pub. Trade time for a stroll through the park on a bar stool. If all the drunks sitting next to you are your mates, try to get a puppy. A little unconditional slobbering love will come a long way. If you're tempted right now, you need to go and find something you can do that doesn't involve alcohol. That can be as simple as going to the library or the park. Do NOT go back to your bar and think you could get away with it. You're going to be all right. You're not going to be all right. Keep away. The places you've been drinking are always off-limits. If you drank at home, your home would have no alcohol, period. Not for celebrations, not for the girlfriend, not for New Years'. If they need a drink from your friend, they should leave the house.

Find a Good Outlet for Stress

Many drinkers, and alcoholics, in particular, have poor coping mechanisms and turn to alcohol in difficult or stressful times.

"It is necessary to establish healthy coping mechanisms to help drug users decompress," says Lena Smith, licensed marriage and family counselor. "Many people find that relaxation, being in nature or exercise of some kind helps to cope with stress when abstaining from alcohol." According to the Passages Addiction Treatment Center in Malibu, California, alternative treatment options include acupressure, massage, acupuncture, art therapy, horsepower, sound therapy, tai chi, and yoga.

Focus on the Benefits

Focusing on your immediate health benefits will enable you to abstain from alcohol withdrawal for the length of your intended time. Keep track of your weight loss and use your heightened energy to exercise.

Enlist Friends, Family or Professionals to Help You

Your social network support will help you abstain. Please visit a psychologist or rehabilitation center if you suspect

you may have an addiction. Use a festive alcohol-free drink, such as a cherry bomb, Shirley Temple, or virgin margarita, if you're attending a party or event.

5.5 Alcoholism vs. Detox centers Drug and Alcohol Rehab

For some people struggling with alcohol addiction, prescription alcoholic treatment is adequate to lead them towards rehabilitation. For others, detox centers, in the long run, are easier, safer, and more effective. In the medication vs. detox center debate, there is no clear winner, but this book will help you decide on your needs the best option.

Medications

A variety of licensed medications are available to help combat alcohol dependence and abuse. However, patients who still consume alcohol do not intend to use any medication. Only if you are currently sober and intend to keep your abstinence from alcohol can you receive a prescription? If you cannot abstain from alcohol on your own, it is possible that you will need a rehabilitation center where you can recover under observation before you receive an alcohol prescription. Keep in mind that every drug comes with possible side effects, so read each drug's following reviews thoroughly. If your doctor thinks you're too risky with a particular medication, you'll have to try another option.

Disulfiram

Disulfiram, also known in some countries as Antabuse and Antabuse, was the first alcohol-approved drug. Before taking this medication, you must abstain from alcohol for at least 12 hours. Patients who use disulfiram, when they consume alcohol, suffer from severe physical reactions. These reactions are very uncomfortable, ranging from nausea and vomiting to mental confusion and breathing difficulty. Usually, reactions start shortly after alcohol consumption and last for at least one hour. While disulfiram is useful in treating alcoholism as opposed to a cure, by creating a negative association, this detox medication discourages drinking. Keep in mind that in rare cases, disulfiram can cause abnormal liver function, which is particularly dangerous in patients whose liver function has already been impaired by alcoholism.

Naltrexone

Naltrexone, a treatment medication, often known as Depade, Revia, or Vivitrol, does not cause unpleasant side effects such as disulfiram. Rather, this medication works by blocking the ability to experience the addictive emotions that alcohol or opiate drugs cause. Naltrexone is intended to be taken after you have abstained from alcohol for a period of time, like disulfiram. Although some people prefer naltrexone over disulfiram because disulfiram is so painful, what can make medicine so effective is the pain? Normally this medication is not as active as preventive drinking. Nonetheless, if your primary drinking purpose is to feel the narcotic effect associated with consuming large amounts of alcohol, it is a useful thing.

Acamprosate

Acamprosate is a relatively new drug for alcohol treatment. This detox medication, unlike naltrexone and disulfiram, does not help you to give up alcohol by punishing you for drinking or preventing you from experiencing the pleasant effects of drinking. Alternatively, by increasing the pain associated with the detoxification process, acamprosate serves as a true detox drug. Although this is certainly a positive thing, some patients prefer disulfiram and naltrexone, as these drugs make drinking less fun, while acamprosate simply makes detoxification less uncomfortable. Nonetheless, if your main reason for drinking is to prevent withdrawal effects, this detox may make a significant difference on your recovery path.

Detox Medication

Naturally, detox centers also recommend a number of medications that make the detoxification process easier to handle. Due to the uncomfortable symptoms associated with the transition to a sober lifestyle, detox centers may be more useful than any prescribed medication if you have trouble with your addiction to alcohol. Detoxification is often so distressing and uncomfortable even with the help of medication such as acamprosate that many patients drink again just to relieve their symptoms. Fortunately, due to a lack of medical supervision, detox centers can prescribe special medicines that you couldn't use at home. There are other ways in which the staff at detox centers can help keep you comfortable if a medication doesn't work. Choosing between prescribed drugs vs. detox center medicines is better if you know that medications are often more effective at detox centers.

Why a Detox Center

In almost every case, detox centers give you the best opportunity to recover from alcohol addiction. Staying in a detox center, however, is not everybody's practical option. If you have children, leaving your house for an extended period of time may be challenging. You can find it difficult to convince them to go to a detox center, even if you have a note from your doctor, depending on your place of work and your relationships with your supervisors. Luckily, the most severe symptoms of withdrawal usually subside after a few days, and if you are unable to remain in a detox center until you have fully recovered, you may be able to stay in the first phase of your recovery process and use a prescription alcohol treatment when you return home.

Why Detox Centers Work

Therapy centers are so effective because they provide unpleasant side effects for patients with drug withdrawal and a supportive environment. The recovery center staff members are used to treat the symptoms of withdrawal, and they will do their best to ensure that your symptoms are reduced with medication. The most positive aspect of a successful detox center, though, is that you are going to go home soberly with no hope of relaxing during the detoxification process, a definite possibility when you rely on a home detox drug.

Chapter 6: Tips that can Change your Life

Breaking the alcohol dependence chains is often one of the most difficult things a person can do. But many of us did not just know how difficult the sobriety of the long term is, but how difficult it can be to take those first steps into your new life.

6.1 If you want to Quit Drinking these are 100+ Tips

- Just try it for 30 days and see how you feel at that time and where you are. I'd have done it much earlier if I knew how much my life would change for the better by giving up booze.

- What's the worst if you're trying? What's the worst if you're not trying?

- You'll soon realize you don't give up anything, but you'll get everything you could ever imagine. Sobriety is not a loss, but energy.

- Don't be afraid to keep you from trying something new.

- C'mon, it's all cool, kids! (Just kidding, I'd just say: what should you lose by trying?) I'd tell them that if they ever want to go there, booze doesn't go anywhere. Or, if they quit, nothing bad will happen, but if they don't, something bad might happen.

- Do it, the longer you wait, the more complicated it will be. The harder it's going to be to discover yourself and the harder it's going to be to face the mirror. 64 Days to count!

- I will base it on my perspective, which is this: I thought about quitting ten years before I finally did it because of REAL, but not true, fear. Each big change is scary, and it's a big change!

- Give it seven days, and be there with it. If it's hell, you could wake up to how profoundly you're dependent on it. If you can make it up to 14 days, you'll start shifting to a cellular level and hopefully start appreciating the fresh insight and power you've got.

- The only thing you miss is the hangover tomorrow!

- You'll soon realize that you don't give up everything, but you'll get everything you've ever dreamed of. Sobriety is energy rather than failure.
- I'd advise you to listen to the gentle voice in your brain, to cultivate it until it's as clear as a bell. Check-in with your mind, body, and soul regularly. And listen to and read Elkhart Tole's A New Planet.

- There's so much trust waiting for you and beyond your wildest dreams. Life was such a fun ride, full

  of adventure, and I guarantee that if I never stopped drinking, it would never have happened.

- One day, try it. How might it hurt? And then the day after and the day after. Does drinking make you happy?

- My darling, you can do it.

- In the eight months, I've been sober, and I think what boils down to for me is that I can now see what alcohol in so many parts of my life have cost me. Alcohol takes us so much more than it ever can give us.

- I know that I was afraid of two things: failure and judgment. On judgment: Sobriety gives you so much courage that by knowing exactly who you are and who you are supposed to be, you conquer everything. And knowing that while drinking, you can't become that guy. When you achieve true sobriety and see all the advantages, no one can

  say shit that annoys you. You realize that you are everybody's most badass! On failure: I'd say to myself and have done it over and over that if you don't try, you'll just fail. You owe it to try it on your own!

- Without alcohol, your life will continue! And you will discover an almost irreplaceable deeper love and understanding of yourself.

- We romanticize our alcohol relationship, and this is one of the most difficult parts. It's like breaking up with a REAL crappy girlfriend and remembering just "the nice." First of all, there's probably a reason you're talking about it. Talk to your intestines. By giving it a try, you have nothing to lose.

- You have a valuable life. Do not encourage more moments of alcohol to take. It's worth leaving.

- If you don't have a drinking problem, you're not going to have a drinking problem.

- You're always going to have a social life that you will not be betrayed by your real friends. That the universe is so much bigger and better than smoking, and you can do so much.

- Throw it all over and see what sticks: meditation, alternative methods of recovery, rest, exercise, sugar, healthy food, therapy, pet therapy, sober friendships. When one thing doesn't work, don't get discouraged!

- It's a decision you're never going to regret. Sometimes you may be dealing with it, but you will never regret it.

- I'd tell them that being sober won't make you dull. You can't see the secrets that booze takes from your life from where you're now. But that's there. Drop the resentment and resistance from fear. Even when it hurts, it's going to get so sweet. It's just waiting.

- Remember to think about it. Trying it is never going to be scary. It's worth it the best I've ever done. There's a big AF people family; you're not alone.

- People in recovery who have gone before you are waiting to cheer you on the other side! It can be terrifying, but it doesn't have to be alone.

- It will take the courage of all kinds. But that's possible. And it's so useful.

- Hear the soul. The heart knows what the brain is unable to comprehend. Be open, be open. Be in lust.

- Without alcohol, your life will continue! And you'll find for yourself a deeper love and understanding that's absolutely irreplaceable.

- Try it and see what's going on for 30 days. I told this to so many friends, and because of the massive improvements in their health and wellbeing, many ended up stopping for good. If you were in drugs and alcohol and like me heavily addicted, be sure to seek medical assistance. Living alcohol-free and drug-free has given me all I ever wanted and so much more!

- Even in small bursts, seek! Try to identify the situation that gives you the most anxiety (like the party of a boozy friend and identify what fear is in that situation like people will think you're boring, and your brain will start to get stronger. I would also say: "Imagine the removal of cotton wool from your face. Life enters into a euphoric yet razor-clear perspective. "I think a great deal of fear about this stems from being nervous that it

  will have to be forever. And that's really overwhelming. It may be just for now to make this decision. Just to try it out. Perhaps a little bit. Even longer. Perhaps forever. Yet take off the burden. It must be "forward" and do it.

- You say "yes" to something else if you say "no" to something else. For me, stopping alcohol created space in my life to fill my career with other awesome things like hobbies, trying new things, etc. Make sure you're drinking REPLACE with something that really excites you and fulfills you. You are going to be much less likely to fall back into old habits. Ask yourself: "What do I want in my life to create space for?" You're more likely outside the bar scene to find satisfying friendships and relationships. Why? And you meet people doing the same things when you're out doing things that interest you, and you have so much more in common with them than most people you meet in a bar. Making new friends while being sober may at first sound daunting, but it's really cool because you don't have to make a connection. It's either there naturally, or it's not there. Sometimes when you really don't, alcohol makes you feel like you have a connection with someone.

- You can save money. Put the money into an account any time you want to drink to save something that would help your life or use it to fly.

- In AA, they say: "We're going to reimburse the suffering." Initially, add hot tea boatloads. And the cream of the ice. Yeah, and there are so many books!

- I don't think I should say that. I would say, "What are you thinking about? "On the contrary. Then by answering a specific concern, you can be more supportive. The apprehension is not to quit; this is the wish. They're afraid of what they might mean. I should assume that the loss of social life and friends or a "relaxation" approach is usually the main factor.

- It's absolutely exhilarating and strong when "no" is used to defend yourself (as in, "no, thanks"), and it feels amazing.

- Play ahead. Imagine never having a hangover to wake up. TODAY AGAIN.

- On the other hand, the happiness you will feel is far beyond what you EVER could imagine.

- Anything I felt I wouldn't be able to do without alcohol (fun, karaoke, dance, feel all right), I could do it and more. When I stop drinking, every aspect of my life improved. I can look in the mirror at myself and feel good about who's looking back.

- You're brave.

- This is when drinking causes pain and harmful consequences for the person: "Yeah, it's hard to give up alcohol, but that's how you live your life as it is now."

- You gain far more social capital than you lose.

- It's made up of stars.

- It's the gift that continues to give, but you must wait for the magic.

- Whenever you want, you can go back to beer. But if it's special, try it and see.

- You get a valuable life. Do not encourage more moments of alcohol to take. It's worth it to leave.
- To your shock, life isn't just as much a challenge as you imagined it. It is possible to enjoy worldly "natural" stuff. You're not meant to loathe

  yourself. You will find your story, your passion, and you will find yourself.

- You know only when you're ready to leave.

- It's all right to be inconvenient.

- It's OK to try. If it's hard, well, you're going to learn something about yourself, at least. And for the better, you're going to grow and improve.

- You're not on your own.

- There's no end to your social life forever. It may be, but not forever, for a moment.

- It's far better than you think it's going to be.

  ALWAYS DO IT. (Nike swoosh style). Try and continue to try. It's as hard as hell, but it's precious the payoff.

- Do you have alcohol? Or you're left out of your life? That's normal to fear change, but a new,

- wonderful life will be experienced by those willing to change. It's not that easy; it is not easy to do anything worthwhile. But it's useful. It's worth it.

- You're going to be all right without it.

- Walk straight into it. Don't take a look back. Repeat until it hangs.

- Commit to a reasonable period of time. You are using resources such as online groups, family, reading articles, counting your money, meditation practice. Do things to be praised, not to be punished punishment results in failure.

- It's not like you think it's going to be you're going to get your freedom back.

- I'd say that fear is blinding us to what the real danger is. In this case, which means that my fear of quitting alcohol would have blinded me to the real danger that I WAS to carry on drinking. Fear is a thief and a liar!

- You're already going home.

- Drinking doesn't make it "better." You won't regret it, even though it's hard to let it go.

- If you're hurting not to do anything that hurts you it's probably an addiction.

- It's much easier than you think!

  Trying will help you start healing from fear and don't try to give your power to fear.

- Try and try again. It's as hard as hell, but it's precious the payoff.

- It can be finished!

-

- Start with small targets of achievement: stay sober for a day, read an article, listen to a sobriety podcast, attend a meeting, speak to a counselor

- It's just terrifying for a while, and then you're going to wonder why you didn't leave sooner.

- All the items you used to "require" liquor, without alcohol, are enjoyable. Just try it a couple of times!

- It feels incredible and strong.

- If you ask me, you'll have something to do with you.

- The other side is GOOD inscrutably!

- You're going to feel a lot better. Give it three months, and you're going to notice a big difference.

- Call it an experiment and see what's going on. Maybe you're surprised!

- I will tell them to read and let Allen Car and Annie Grace talk to your unconscious mind. Then commit to yourself say thirty or sixty days, then see how you feel. And write down it! The second wish, I wrote down more. And get funding. So important, so important.

- I really had to ask myself if alcohol was good for me. Has this added value to my life? The reply was no. Without it, I had to decide that I was all right.

- You don't have to do it on your own.

- There's a lot of life waiting for you beyond fear.

- It's the hardest and strongest decision I've ever made to stop drinking. Never take a look back.

- You ought to be afraid. It's frightening. There are so many ways that your life can change. Some of it will suck, but you will feel all the emotions and wake up one day, and you will understand true happiness for the first time in years and feel alive, and you will not want to go back to the way things are.

- Congratulations on reaching this point! Be kind to you. Take the pressure off for the first time to get it together. You should try as many times as you want to be sober. Start and see how you're going for 30 days. Each day you are sober, thank yourself. The cravings are hopefully going to stop. Sober life is amazing.

- It's great to find out how much better you can do when you take alcohol out of your body!

- Continuing to drink is likely to be as terrifying as sobriety, if not more so.

- Continue to try. Hot night baths. Instagram's books and people who do dry life. Continue to try.

- It's all right to be scared. Either way, do it.

- All the items you used to "require" liquor, without alcohol, are enjoyable. Just try it a couple of times!
- You've been killed by alcohol, brush.

- You can do anything if you can get through the first weekend.

- The reason to stop having more influence than any excuse that holds you back.

- Are you scared of the days, the restful sleep, and the recollection of events? If not, then go forthat.

- It's important. If you relapse, don't be that hard on yourself, just try again.

- Take my hand here.

- If you ask yourself the question, something already knows the answer within your heart.

- Reach a point when you're not thinking about alcohol. Security!

- Whether you stay sober or not, you will still have some alcohol-related knowledge for yourself. A test is always worth it.

- The first step toward self-love is sobriety.

- Focus on creating healthier new habits and hanging with people who have other hobbies than eating and drinking.
- You'll never know if you've ever tried it. (Hint:

  Even if it takes 1 or 20 tries, it's always worth it.)
  • Anxiety will make it easier for more days to add up, trust yourself. You're very brave, and you're going to be surprised by your own strength.

- Soak up and I mean, SOAK YOURSELF in the Instagram realm of pro-sobriety. This survivor group is the saviors of each other including yours.

- It's as tough as hell. The withdrawals, like hell, are terrible. Due to physical, emotional, and spiritual torment, you will want to die EVERY MINUTE. Get medical assistance to remove safely It's free. But once you step off the abuse hamster wheel, it's OK. You'll be able to look back and realize that life isn't hopeless like anything painful and hard. It's full of hope and potential. Through satisfying ways, you will be able to practice presence and perception. Things you didn't think are possible are actually true. Drop-in positive support in these first stages of breaking the chains of addiction. It's going to take some days for a village to get through those days accepting all the support you can. You're going to break those guilt and shame chains. It's worth it. Without hard work, there is no success.

- The further you sit back and think about everything, the more disturbing it "looks" from your mind's perspective. The body is strong and is capable of doing incredible things. Start one day at a time and bear in mind a realistic goal. If you can find a buddy to share with you, you can feel less lonely and sometimes enjoy motivating each other.

- The physical reward I still begin with: no more hangovers. That seems to intimidate the lease when you get started first.

- Attend the meeting of the AA! Hearing the stories of other people can really open your eyes.

- Focus on creating healthier new habits and hanging with people who have other hobbies than eating and drinking.

- You don't get to drink anymore. It's you've never had to.

- Only YOU can make the bold decision to stop drinking at the end of the day. But if you do, you ought to know you're not alone. And you're going to recover just like so many of us. And yes, recovery is a lifetime operation, but we guarantee that you will be grateful for it in the end.

Chapter 7: How to Stop being an Alcoholic?

Are you wondering how you can handle an intoxicated mother during the holidays or how you can help her? Have you been told by friends that you are your spouse's enabler? Do you suffer the consequences of the alcohol problem of a loved one? It can be hard to hear that when a loved one struggles with addiction; you need to improve yourself. It's their problem after all, isn't it? Unfortunately, you can only improve yourself, and the only way to change the current course of your interactions with people with substance abuse problems is to change your reactions.

Those of us who reside or have resided among active addicts or those who struggle with dependence feel that the encounter has influenced them deeply. Sometimes, your own actions and choices will cause frustration and pressure. You can put it in a different perspective by changing your approach and attitude to the issue so that it no longer consumes your thoughts and your life. To some extent, it is rewarding to realize that you can change your mindset and attitude. You don't have to keep doing some of the stuff you do with a person with an addiction to your dance.

7.1 If you Love an Alcoholic (Try these suggestions)

Blaming Yourself

Sad wife and crazy husband. It is characteristic of alcoholics to try to blame conditions or others around them, including those closest to them. Hearing an addict claim, "The only reason I'm drinking is because of you" Don't buy into it. If your loved one is really an addict, no matter what you do or do, he's going to drink. It's not the fault of you. He's become alcohol-dependent, and nothing will get between him and his favorite drug.

Taking It Personally

If alcoholics vow never to drink again, but a short time later they return to drink, as usual, it is convenient for members of the family to personally embrace the broken promises and lies. You might think, "If she loves me so much. she wouldn't lie to me." But if she's become really addicted to alcohol, she may have changed her brain chemistry to the point that she's totally surprised by some of the choices she makes. She may not have influence over her own decision-making.

Try to Control It

Many alcoholic family members naturally try their best to get their loved ones to stop drinking. Sadly, it usually results in feeling lonely and disappointed by the family members of the alcoholic. You may say to yourself that you can certainly do something, But the reality is that even alcoholics cannot regulate their drink, try as much as they can. Despite realizing you might just want to help the loved addict in the middle of a crisis. In fact, this is usually the time when there is nothing the family should do.

When an alcoholic or substance addict reaches a point of crisis, this is sometimes the moment the person finally recognizes that he has a problem and starts to look for help. However, if friends or family rush into the crisis situation and "rescue" the individual, the determination to get support can be postponed and "rescue" the person from the crisis situation, the decision to get help can be postponed.

Let a Crisis Happen

It is very difficult for those who love addiction to sit back and let the crisis play its fullest role. If abusers reach the point of substance abuse when they get a DUI, lose their job, or get thrown into jail, knowing that the best thing they can do in the case is to do nothing is a difficult concept for their loved ones. It seems to go against all they think. It causes the loop, sadly, to continue. Forever.

They don't have to create a crisis, but learning detachment will allow you to create a crisis that could be the only way to change.

Try to Cure It

Make no mistake; alcoholism or dependence on alcohol is a primary, chronic, and progressive disease that can sometimes be fatal. You are not a healthcare professional, and you should not bear the responsibility to handle friends or family members, even if you are. You are not a trained counselor for substance abuse, and your role should not be a counselor again, also if you are. You just love someone who will need professional treatment to get well still. That is the responsibility of the addict, not yours. You can't cure illness. Whatever your history may be, you need support from outside.

Alcoholics typically go through a couple of stages before they are willing to change. Until an alcoholic begins to contemplate quitting, resistance will often meet with any actions you take to "help" her left.

Although it is not your duty to "heal" the addiction of your loved one, you might want to know some of the stuff drinkers wish to leave, as well as some of the things that make an alcoholic stay sober. You may want to seek an intervention from your parents. Spend some time reading on how to take care of yourself by finding ways not for yourself to prepare an operation, but because it is often the only way a person with an addiction can get the support they need.

Covering it Up

There's a joke about an addict in denial in rehab circles who cries, "I don't have an issue, so don't tell anybody!" Typically, alcoholics don't want anyone to know the level of their alcohol consumption because if someone sees the full extent of the problem, they may try to help. When family members seek to "support" (alcoholic enable) by covering up for their drinking and making excuses for it, they play right into the blame trap of the alcoholic. The best approach is to deal with the problem openly and honestly.

Accepting Unacceptable Behavior

Acceptance of unacceptable behavior usually begins with a small incident that brushes family members with, "They just had too much to drink." And the next time the behavior gets worse and worse. You start accepting more and more unacceptable behavior gradually. Before you know it, you will find yourself in an abusive relationship.

It is never necessary to rape. In your life, you don't have to accept unacceptable behavior. You've got choices.

Protecting your kids from unacceptable behavior is also essential. Do not tolerate any comments that are harmful or negative to your children. Such remarks can lead to permanent harm to the psyche of a child. Protect your kids, and don't hesitate to keep your kid away from someone who drinks and doesn't respect your limits. It can leave lasting wounds to grow up in an alcoholic family.

Having Unreasonable Expectations

The difficulty with an alcoholic is that, under certain circumstances, what might seem like a reasonable expectation might be irrational for an addict. If alcoholics swear to you and themselves that they will never touch another drop, you might expect them to be sincere and not drink again. But this presumption turns out to be unrealistic for alcoholics. Will it be fair to expect someone to be truthful to you when you cannot evenbe real with yourself or yourself?

Living in the Past

Its best way of dealing with depression in the family is to remain focused on the current situation. Alcoholism is a progressive disease. It doesn't reach a certain level and stays there for a very long time; it keeps getting worse until the alcoholic is seeking help. You can't allow past deceptions and errors to influence your decisions today because conditions are likely to have changed.

Enabling

When trying to "help," well-meaning loved ones frequently do something that encourages alcoholics to proceed down their destructive paths. Find out what makes this happen and make sure you don't do anything that promotes the denial of the addict or keeps them from facing the inevitable consequences of their actions. When they realized that their enabling system was no longer in place, many an alcoholic finally reached out for help. Take this quiz for a moment to see if you're supporting an alcoholic.

Which happens if you encourage an alcoholic to do so? The exact answer depends on the particular situation, but what usually happens is that: the addict never feels the pain. This takes the focus away from the actions of the alcoholic. For example, if your loved one walks through the yard and you gently help him into the house and bed, you just feel the pain. Then the focus becomes what you have done moved him as opposed to what he has done, which is going out. In this case, as he wakes up in the morning on the lawn, With the neighbors opening the window and entering the house, while you and the children are happy to eat breakfast, the suffering is left to them. The only thing he has gone to face is his behavior. In other words, his behavior becomes the focus instead of your reaction to his practice. He will only feel a need to improve once he feels his suffering.

Natural consequences can mean you refuse to stay with the alcoholic at any time. For the alcoholic, this is not being mean or unkind, but instead being self-protective. It is not your responsibility to "heal" your loved one's alcoholism. Still, one aspect that can move a person from the pre-contemplative stage to the contemplative stage of overcoming addiction is to allow natural outcomes to occur. That contemplative stage finishes with the decision to change, but before the dependency is managed, more measures such as planning, intervention, and future maintenance and probable relapse are usually needed.

Putting off Getting Help

After years of alcoholic cover-up and not talking about the "problem" outside the family, it may seem daunting to seek advice from a support group such as Al-Anon Family Groups. Yet millions of people have found solutions in those meetings that contribute to serenity. Moving to a meeting with Al-Anon was one of those things you say, "I should have done this years ago."

Prescription of Recovery

July 2013 edition of the newsletter "DMC Campfire" included an article about addicted families entitled "How can I help" The report included what DMC calls a "Guaranteed Recovery Prescription. "Although they are targeted at Christian families struggling with addiction, the concepts can be applied by all: forgiving yourself means being able to say many things, including you no longer have to deny addiction in your life.

- You no longer have to use the addict to monitor it.
- You do not need to save the abuser anymore.

- You no longer need to be interested in the abuser's motives. You no longer have to make assurances or remove them.
- You no longer have to ask the uninformed for advice.
- You don't need to nag, lecture, threaten, or talk anymore.
- You don't have to let the addict manipulate you or your kids anymore.
- You don't have to be an addiction victim anymore.

Look After Yourself

There may be very little that you can do to support the addict until he or she is ready for help, but you may stop letting the problem of drinking consume your thoughts and your life. Making choices that are good for your own mental and physical health is all right.

Chapter 8: The Benefits of Not an Alcoholic

What is not drinking alcohol's benefits?

Quitting drinking may sound extreme, but these legit health benefits of sobering might convince you to put your beer down.

This is partially due to an increased awareness of excessive alcohol consumption: "alcohol use disorder" in young women is on the rise, and there has been an increase in the number of young adults suffering from alcohol-driven liver disease and cirrhosis." Its U.S. Task Force on Preventive Services has just announced that its primary care doctors will monitor all adults, including pregnant women, for excessive alcohol use during checkups, according to a new statement from the medical journal JAMA. And, well, more and more research show that even moderate alcohol use is not safe for your wellbeing-never mind binge drinking's dire health consequences.

Although it may sound a bit radical, there are a lot of advantages to giving up alcohol temporarily.

8.1 A healthy lifestyle

You see Better

How different they look is one of the first things people who stop drinking notes. The liver starts to break down alcohol and releases a toxic by-product of acetaldehyde that dries the skin and dehydrates other tissues of the body. Nonetheless, red skin and a flushed face after a few drinks are not the only drawbacks. Alcohol also causes inflammation, so that more blackheads, whiteheads, and general breakouts can occur in your swollen blood capillaries.

If alcohol causes more clogged pores to develop in your skin, untreated acne may turn into cysts or lesions, resulting in permanent scarring. You might already be struggling with your skin. If so, there may be some unexpected wonders to stop drinking. Within the first week of not drinking, your lighter tint would probably surprise you and those around you.

You feel Better

Imagine under your eyes no more headaches, dry mouths, and dark circles. People who stop drinking show lower levels of blood sugar and cholesterol, more energy all day long, and improved focus and work efficiency.

Even if you're not a regular drinker, a weekend in the pub or a few glasses of wine every night can still hurt your health and mental capacity. Abstaining allows you to see just how much alcohol is impeding your daily performance and how much better without it, you can feel.

Control over your Emotions

While people turn to liquor to take their minds away from their problems, alcohol can intensify depression and anxiety. Research by the School of Medicine at the University of North Carolina showed that alcohol could rewire the neural pathways of the brain and make people more vulnerable to anxiety issues.

The tendency to go hand in hand with addiction and mental health issues. If you suffer from depression or anxiety, it is easy to become addicted to the initial calming effects of alcohol. Unfortunately, over time, drinking builds up tolerance and ultimately weakens the reward system of your brain. You want more and more drinks to feel good, but you will never look as good as you used to if you first started to drink.

A large part of alcoholic rehabilitation understands that there are other ways of dealing with mental problems. The creation of affirming and positive solutions for stress and negative emotions makes it possible for people to become more resilient without alcohol and lead more productive lives.

Your Mental Health Improves

Alcohol is a depressant that can upset the chemistry of our brain and leave us emotionally unbalanced. The consequences of drinking can be harmful to people who already have a mental health issue associated with brain chemistry, such as Major Depressive Disorder or Generalized Anxiety Disorder.

It's natural to feel more comfortable and less stressed after a few drinks, but self-medication with alcohol will make us feel worse every time we wear our buzz. It's Lowered serotonin levels after drinking aggravate depression and alcohol-related mood swings that cause us to experience painful memories and unresolved feelings while being intoxicated. Such emotions make us just want to drink more.

People with mental health problems are more likely to suffer from addiction. Quitting alcohol leads to the right path to better mental health and enhanced selfawareness.

You can lose weight and get stronger. People who drink every day can eat hundreds or thousands of extra calories every week. There is no nutritional value for alcohol, so the "vacuum calories" you always hear about are empty. In reality, the body wants to remove alcohol, so instead of reducing fats or carbohydrates and sugars, it is more likely to focus on that.

Cutting back on alcohol or quitting will reduce your caloric intake dramatically and help you feel healthier. Taking up a daily exercise routine is also a great time, And, when slimming down, you can turn your thoughts and resources into something positive.

You Sleep Better

Alcohol helps many people fall asleep, but it does not help them to sleep better. Increased sleep disturbances lead to lower sleep quality for drinkers than non-drinkers.

More time spent in the REM sleep period means that our bodies are not as recovered and refreshed as they might be every morning. Lack of proper sleep can also contribute throughout the day to memory problems, concentration problems, reduced cognitive performance, and increased fatigue.

Lower Risk of Developing Cancer

You have probably heard that consuming small amounts of alcohol will help prevent heart problems and disease, but it can do the same to stop drinking. Drinking has been associated with various types of cancer, including cancer of the liver, cancer of the intestine, and cancer of the head and neck.

Alcohol does not in itself cause cancer (carcinogenic). However, a study conducted by the Medical Research Council Molecular Biology Laboratory, Cambridge, showed how alcohol and acetaldehyde could cause white blood cell breakdown and alter sequences of DNA that increase the likelihood of cancer.

More Time to Focus

You won't have to waste your mornings sleeping off a hangover or lose your nights at another pub session. You should invest your resources in spending quality time with family and friends, trying a new hobby, and improving yourself as an individual rather than structuring your social calendar around alcohol.

Have Better Sex

It's a misconception that alcohol is an aphrodisiac. In reality, your sexual performance may be harmed by alcohol. Drinking was associated with erectile dysfunction, dryness in the uterus, and decreased sensitivity. You are less likely to make impulsive decisions without alcohol in the mix as well. It means you're less likely to have sex with someone you don't know.

Don't Have fewer mood swings

As we explained earlier, alcohol can alter our brain chemistry and cause extreme reactions. Also contributing to greater conflict is the correlation between alcohol and aggressive behavior, which harms our ties. You can enjoy a more stable mindset when you are sober and focus on acting from reason to pure emotional response.

Brain Performance

Drinking is taking a toll on our cognitive performance so that it can lead to better concentration, productivity, and safer, all-round life. The frontal lobe is most likely to be affected by alcohol addiction, and the regeneration of brain cells will continue for years after you stop drinking. You will enjoy better memory, greater behavioral control, emotional regulation, and problem-solving abilities as your brain boosts back and you rewire critical alcoholfree neural pathways.

Save more Money

With many people spending more than £ 50,000 on alcohol throughout their lives, it's safe to say that quitting your wallet will do wonders. Consider putting the money you save into a good cause or an individual savings account that can go into a dream holiday.

Control Over Your Drinking

If you give up drinking for a short time-saying through a Dry January-style challenge-you may have an impact on your drinking habits long afterward. (If the benefits persuade you to ditch booze-even for a while-follow these tips on how to stop drinking alcohol without feeling all the FOMO. The University of Sussex's new research tracked more than 800 people who participated in Dry January 2018 and found that in August, participants also drank less. That total number of drinking days fell from
4.3 a week to 3.3, the average rate of drinking decreased from 3.4 per month to 2.1 per month, and 80 participants indicated a greater sense of control over their drinking.

"Dry January's brilliant thing is that it's not even January," psychologist Richard de Visser, who led the research team, said in a statement. "Being alcohol-free for 31 days teaches us that we don't need alcohol to have fun, to relax, to socialize. That means we're better able to make choices about our drinking for the rest of the year and to avoid slipping into drinking more than we want."

Better Health

"Alcohol doesn't only contain a lot of empty calories, but when people drink too much, they tend to drink too much. Proof: 58 percent of participants in the Dry January study of the University of Essex reported losing weight after giving up alcohol for just one month. "Getting hungover also has things like walking for a morning run or going to the gym. People are much better able to stick with their habits by giving it up," she says. "There are, of course, long-term benefits in terms of reducing the risk of many cancers, improving heart health, strengthening the immune system, and not harming the liver." (For example, only one serving of alcohol per day can raise the risk of breast cancer.) You can find a complete rundown of the risks associated with alcohol on the National Institute for Alcohol Abuse and Alcoholism website.

Better Sleep

"As a psychologist, so many of my patients report having trouble sleeping," Dr. MacMillan says. When it comes to poor sleep, alcohol is like pouring salt on a wound. It inhibits REM sleep (the most restorative period of rest) and wreaks havoc with circadian rhythms. When people give up alcohol, their rest will benefit tremendously and, in effect, improves their overall mental health. "Here is some about how you sleep with alcohol. Over 70% of the students participated by the end of Dry January.

Better Moods

If you're sleeping better, you're likely to feel more energized-but that's not the only reason why you can increase your energy by quitting alcohol. "Taking a break from booze can raise your energy levels," says a registered dietitian nutritionist, Kristin Koskinen, R.D.N. Drinking weakens your vitamin B supply (which is critical for sustained energy). "The B vitamins, like most nutrients, have not just one purpose so that you may notice an impact with alcohol consumption on both your energy and mood," she says. That's possibly one explanation why the University of Sussex study recorded that 67 percent of Dry January participants had more fuel.

Better Skin

"The removal of alcohol from your diet can improve your appearance," Koskinen says. "We've all heard that alcohol is dehydrated. Having skin cells lose plumpness, allowing them to become stressed, Hair that looks older. "Yes, the Sussex University study found that 54% of Dry January participants reported better skin.

Faster Recovery "

Alcohol can affect hydration status, motor skills, and muscle recovery from an athletic performance perspective," notes Angie Asche, R.D., a sports dietitian and clinical exercise physiologist. "Evidence has shown that alcohol consumption can potentially magnify delayed muscle soreness DOMS after strenuous workouts by slowing down the recovery process and through Wailing. Drugs can make it impossible for athletes to see the results they want with such negative effects on their workouts on body composition and muscle recovery."

Dealing with your Questions

"Converting to alcohol to cope with stressful or unpleasant feelings means people are not able to cope with healthy coping strategies or taking steps to cope with those feelings, "Dr. MacMillan says," says Dr. MacMillan. "If alcohol is eliminated as an option, people can take their kidneys back to their mental health and find more efficient ways to get through their days." (And when you start drinking binge at a young age, it can further impair your ability to cope with feelings in a healthy manner. Only squeezing alcohol for a short time will shed some light on how you can use alcohol to cope with it

More Confidence

Yes, definitely. To help them get through social situations, most people rely on alcohol to make them unhappy. Holler, if you're one of the many people with social anxiety. "If alcohol is no longer there as a crutch, it can be hard to adjust at first. However, in the long run, without it, people can gain skills and believe they can actually connect with others in a constructive and friendly way Respectful, Dr. MacMillan says. "It can feel powerful and contribute to more honest interactions with others without the so-called' to distort interactions." Trust: 71% of Dry January participants reported in the University of Sussex study that they did not need a drink to enjoy themselves.

Stay Fit

Alcohol is a significant source of empty calories, including Cheetos and donuts. The body simply retains the excess fat of its sugars. Not only does juice not add vitamins or minerals, but it also prevents nutrient absorption from other sources. Your body can absorb vitamin C, thiamin, vitamin B12, folic acid, and zinc when you stop drinking.

In particular, binge drinking has proved to be a problem for people with weight problems. If you have to maintain weight goals, you'll find it much easier if you're sober to stay on track. Exercise can help, but as consumption rises, the effectiveness of working out decreases. Alcohol significantly depresses your metabolism and muscle regeneration, putting your stamina and the ability to convert carbohydrates into usable energy into a big dent.

All of this shows the significant benefits of stopping drinking. Without alcohol, your exercise will give you more fitness. You'll be more satisfied with your workouts. Through the day you'll have more energy, and at night you'll get more restful sleep. When you try to lose weight, it will make the process much simpler. You're going to be a happier, more resilient person.

Be Disease-Free

Alcohol consumption is charming, but it is also a significant factor contributing to over 60 different conditions. This affects the body relatively violently, increasing the risk of a variety of illnesses, cardiovascular diseases, and cognitive disorders. The International Cancer Research Agency categorizes alcohol as a carcinogen in Group 1.

Because it accelerates the brain's shrinkage, the longterm use of alcohol is correlated with later-life dementia growth. Its typically rude central nervous system disruption makes it a risk factor for high blood pressure, and hence for kidney disease, heart disease, and stroke. It also increases susceptibility to infectious diseases and types II diabetes, and in large quantities, it can cause nerve damage.

On the other hand, it is almost entirely possible to feel the positive effects of stopping alcohol. You will have improved liver function, cholesterol in the blood, and balance of blood sugar. Your immune system will also thank you; among other preventable diseases, you will have a natural resistance to the common cold.

If you have wounds or the need for physical rehabilitation, under the influence of a sober lifestyle, your body can heal more quickly. When you try to get pregnantyou're, you can praise practically overnight for boosting your fertility. And who's in need of them? Then you would be shocked how well your body works if you're not forced to undergo prolonged periods of dehydration.

The relationship between alcohol and sex has always been awkward. We seem to meet up more frequently in the presence of each other on the one side. Those hookups, on the other hand, are not always completely satisfying.

Alcohol can sometimes boost your libido, but at the same time, it tends to diminish your ability to act on the impulse. As a consequence, dudes are often unable to' get it together.' Ladies lose responsiveness. You may find that not only is it easier to have sober sex when you stop drinking. It's also much more enjoyable.

Not to mention, people who drink more are involved in riskier sexual activities, so much so that alcohol triples their chances of getting a nasty STD relative to sober people. Protection is also less likely to be used. That's because it does several things about your ability to judge and make decisions.

If you're like most people, the benefits of stopping drinking might include a fall in the sheer amount of intercourse and a significant improvement in the quality of your sex life. Quitting drinking, in short, means more orgasms, fewer crabs, and fewer unwanted pregnancies. This is a win-win.

Be Smarter

Life is a fun, demanding game that requires a person to think on their feet. In this regard, alcohol will not help but will quit. Since alcohol tends to have a dull effect on one's senses and brainwork, it has the potential to clarify your outlook to stop drinking seriously. You're going to be able to think better, getting rid of something that makes learning and creating new memories much harder.

Alcohol can have lifelong negative cognitive effects, even if you are not intoxicated. Having at least five alcoholic drinks a night will affect your brain's goings-on for up to three days. This is why a sober lifestyle is more effective than trying to cram in between episodes of drunkenness your' smart' moments.

Feel Better

Just as alcohol hurts higher cognition, it also disrupts the mood and emotions of an individual. Under the direct influence of alcohol, feelings appear to be more "myopic" or intense, but even during drinking sessions, there may be a distortion of feeling in some people that leads to depression.

Numbness can alternate with bouts of rage, sorrow, or remorse, even among people who do not see themselves as alcoholics. The effects of heavy drinking can be drastic and even aggressive for those with severe anger management problems. The drama can easily spill into their romantic or family life for those in intimate relationships.

For maximum emotional stability, you can be sober. Sobriety allows you to feel consistently in the right way, not too much or too little. You are yet feeling fine when sober can come even more comfortable for those who drink to feel better.

8.2 Benefits for Health

A Healthier Brain

Alcohol inhibits the interaction between neurons and brain neurotransmitters, which are the control mechanisms for all primary body functions such as breathing, thought, talking, and walking. Alcohol consumption can severely damage the cerebellum, cerebral cortex, brain tissue, And the network of limbs. Such damage can lead to multiple problems, including reduced brain cells, depression, changes in mood, poor sleep, and alcohol dependence.

Stronger Immune System

Alcohol damages the immune system and makes combating illness and disease more difficult for the body. Alcohol decreases white blood cells ' efficacy in destroying harmful bacteria. Heavy drinkers are more vulnerable to infectious diseases such as hepatitis or pneumonia. However, up to 24 hours after the drinking episode, even one instance of heavy drinking may expose the body to infection. Stopping drinking will improve the ability of the body to combat infections immediately.

A Healthier Liver

It is the liver's responsibility to break down alcohol that dispenses horrible toxins. Over time, the use of alcohol can cause the liver to become overwhelmed with toxins and fat build-up, leading to steatosis, or "fatty liver," which is an early sign of liver disease.

A fatty liver can cause hepatitis, fibrosis, and cirrhosis. A

Merck Manuals study shows that under certain circumstances, liver damage can be reversed, with even fatty liver showing complete resolution within six weeks.

It is not possible to change any results, such as fibrosis and cirrhosis. Drug treatment can improve the overall health of the liver and boost the removal of toxins in the skin.

Stronger Heart

Regularly or even on one occasion, drinking copious amounts of alcohol can damage your heart and weaken your muscles. This damage can result in heart disease, strokes, diabetes, arrhythmias of the chest. Through. Heavy alcohol use and avoiding alcohol-related heart damage, including heart attacks, people can improve the health of their cardiovascular systems.

Decreased Risk of Cancer

Drug harms antibodies that prevent tumor cells and puts a person at a much higher risk of cancer than they usually would.

As per the American Public Health Journal, alcohol causes 3.5% cancer deaths in America, or about 20,000 cancerrelated deaths each year. We also say, "It is important to reduce alcohol consumption and under- emphasized strategy for cancer prevention." Drinking alcohol is associated with many cancers, including cancer of the head and neck, cancer of the esophagus, cancer of the breast, liver, and colorectal cancer. Stopping drinking now can significantly reduce the risk of developing such diseases for an individual.

Improved Digestion

The pancreas may be impaired by regular alcohol intake, which is essential for proper digestion. Alcohol prevents the absorption of vitamins and nutrients in the small intestines and can cause chronic vomiting, nausea, and anorexia in people who drink heavily. Alcohol consumption enhances the transfer of toxins through the intestinal walls. Once alcohol is avoided, all these adverse gastrointestinal effects can be reduced.

Improved Memory

Centrist for heavy alcohol use is associated with brain reduction in brain shrinkage, especially in the cognitive and learning-related areas. Memory impairments are seen with only a few drinks, and the amount of alcohol consumed increases, this memory lapses. According to the National Alcohol Abuse and Alcoholism Institute, abstaining from alcohol for several months or longer can enable partial correction of structural brain changes due to drinking, including reversal of negative impacts on thinking skills, issue-solving, memory, and attention.

Your Health is in Your Hands

These seven are not limited to the benefits of ceasing alcohol use, especially binge drinking. Although some damage may be irreversible, the body of everybody is different and can be repaired to some extent. The main objective of abstaining from alcohol is to prevent further damage.

If you are Trying to Quit Alcohol

- Enhanced concentration and problem-solving

- Increased mental focus and improved memory function

- Enhanced digestion and elimination of harmful toxins

- Increased absorption of vitamins and minerals

- Weight loss due to lower caloric

Benefits of Quitting Alcohol

Those who suffer from the morning's bleary-eyed, headin - a-vise migraine because they know the alcohol's extreme toxicity.

Weddings are, of course, incomplete without champagne toasts, and with the addition of a few cocktails, office parties become just a bit more interesting.

Or do the health risks outweigh the benefits to your social life? Just how difficult is it without a few drinks to survive?

Those who suffered from the morning's bleary-eyed, head-in - a-vise migraine despite recognizing the alcohol's extreme toxicity. But some symptoms go beyond the hangover.

The use and abuse of alcohol increase the risk of cancer, pancreatitis, digestive problems, cardiovascular problems, stroke, depression, anxiety, and dementia in many forms. Moreover, consistent alcohol use depletes neurotransmitters and changes the function of the brain.

There are several immediate improvements in health after the cessation of alcohol. This is from a recent scientist's report. Liver fat fell by 15 percent after just one month of non-drinking. Blood glucose levels dropped by 16 percent, and cholesterol decreased by five percent. Also, the sleep quality and concentration ability of the participants improved significantly.

Save your Brain

Your liver is not the only organ that is at risk from consistent heavy drinking. "Heavy drinking can have serious and far-reaching effects on the brain, ranging from minor declines in memory to persistent and worsening disorders requiring lifelong custody care," according to the National Institute on Alcohol Abuse and Alcoholism (NIAAA). Only moderate drinking may cause memory lapses, and at the other extreme, binge drinking may lead to severe memory loss. However, even alcoholics who have already experienced cognitive impairment within a year of abstinence can regain at least some brain function.

Giving up booze can also help the growth of new brain cells, as large amounts of alcohol can slow or stop new brain cells from growing. It is this lack of growth that leads to long-term deficits in crucial brain areas.

Furthermore, alcohol abuse can lead to thiamine deficiency, leading to severe brain disorders such as Wernicke-Korsakoff syndrome (WKS).

Abstinence will Save your Waistline

Good news if you want to lose a few pounds: avoiding drinking encourages weight loss for women in particular. Most forms of alcohol, when processed by the body, are loaded with sugar or become sugars.

Registered nurse Travis Patrick says, "Drinking bursts of estrogen for women, which encourages the accumulation of fat in the belly. Alcohol abstinence has a myriad of health benefits that are immediately felt. "Research shows that alcohol creates additional physical effects on women. Faster than intoxicated men, alcoholic women develop liver cirrhosis, heart muscle damage, or cardiomyopathy and nerve damage.

Improve your Mood

You might have learned that alcohol is a depressant. You may even have had a slump the next day. But beyond that, alcohol can interfere with brain function and activity of the brain cell and neurotransmitter, leading to brain damage, anxiety, and even suicidal thoughts.

According to Alcohol Research & Health, a liver disease arising from alcohol consumption may harm the brain, contributing to a severe and potentially fatal neurological disorder known as emesis. This disease triggers sleep cycle disturbance, personality changes, mood swings, depression, and reduced attention span.

Conclusion:

The fantastic news is that there are many health benefits about stop drinking for a week, a month, or even a year. The bad news is that can be difficult to abstain from alcohol, particularly in social situations.

Individuals sometimes conceal or deny that they have a problem with their drinking. Whether you are in trouble or someone you know, how can you say? Signs of a possible problem include getting friends or relatives expressing concern, here are a few tips for helping you achieve abstinence from alcohol, and thinking you should cut but be unable to do so, and wanting a morning drink to calm your nerves or alleviate a hangover.

Many people with drinking problems are working hard to solve them, and these people are often able to recover on their own with the help of family members or friends. Those with alcohol dependence, however, will usually not stop drinking alone through willpower. Many needs help from outside. To avoid life-threatening withdrawal symptoms such as seizures, they may need medically supervised detoxification. When people are stable, they may need help to resolve the psychological problems associated with drinking problems.

There are several ways to deal with alcohol problems. For all people, no one approach is best. Alcohol is not a product standard. While it carries connotations of enjoyment and sociability in the minds of many, its use has numerous and widespread harmful consequences.

If you are knee-deep in a deluge of alcohol, it can be difficult to imagine life without it. However, it is a mirage. There are many benefits of stopping drinking; we have just scratched the surface here. While there is nothing wrong with indulging once in a while, leave alcohol behind, and you'll soon find that without drinking life is not only possible, it's far, far better.

Nonetheless, there is a lot of help available. There are facilities for detoxification and much more. You will consider it if you ask for help. If the first aid does not work, keep trying, there are even medications available that support prevents alcohol by triggering painful physical reactions. If you need to stop drinking so you can regain control of your life, this book will help you to get back on track, covering many tips to stop drinking.

References:

1-   How to Safely Detox From Alcohol at Home. (2019). Retrieved from https://www.therecoveryvillage.com/alcoholabuse/w ithdrawal-detox/safely-detox-alcohol-home/

2-   Self-help strategies for quitting drinking - Rethinking Drinking - NIAAA. (2019). Retrieved from https://www.rethinkingdrinking.niaaa.nih.gov/ Thi nki ng-about-a-change/Support- forquitting/Self-Help-Strategies-For-Quitting.aspx

3-   Dave Asprey Blog. (2019). Alcohol Addiction: How to Quit Drinking for Good. [online] Available at: https://blog.daveasprey.com/how-to-quit-drinking/.

4-   Australian Government Department of Health. (2019).

5-   reduce or quit alcohol? [online] Available at: https://www.health.gov.au/health-topics/alcohol/about-alcohol/how-can-you-reduce- orquit-alcohol.

6-   Alcoholism - Statistics, Hereditary & Symptoms | Everyday Health. (2019). Retrieved from https://www.everydayhealth.com/alcoholism/gui de/

7-   Benefits of Sobriety | Why stop drinking? | Your First Step. (2019). Retrieved from https://yourfirststep.org/benefits-of-sobriety/

8-   Medical News Today. (2019). Giving up alcohol for just 1 month has lasting benefits. [online] Available at: https://www.medicalnewstoday.com/articles/324 079 .php.

9-   Healthfully. (2019). Retrieved from https://healthfully.com/the-benefits-of-quittingalcohol-and-how-to-do-it-10851766.html

10-   Open Learn. (2019). Alcohol and human health.

[online] Available at:

https://www.open.edu/openlearn/science-mathstechnology/science/biology/alcohol-and- humanhealth/content-section-1.5.

Gambling Addiction

The Easy Guide to Stop Gambling, Understand What's Behind Your Addiction and Learn How to Terminate It Now

Chapter 1: An Introduction to Gambling

Gambling has been defined in a number of ways. The definitions we find in dictionaries and other scholarly articles do vary in their selection of words. Still, contextually, they converge on one single-most critical fact, that is, gambling entails betting or staking or risking or jeopardizing or endangering something of value in anticipation of future monetary (or any other tangible) outcome contingent upon mere chance or accident. In short, gambling may be best described as putting your precious things in danger in the hope of uncertain future benefits. This process can be preceded by calculations or by taking the lead from past results, but they do not lend authenticity to the process and its outcome. Thus, gambling heinous and perilous pervasiveness in today's world has become irrational and questionable from both the point of gamblers and the people advocating and patronizing this activity.

The results of gambling games can be decided by chance alone, either through the random activity of a tossed pair of dice or ball on a roulette wheel, or through physical ability, preparation, or prowess in athletic competitions, or a combination of strategy and chance. The rules that govern gambling games often misrepresent the relationship between the game's components, which depends on ability and chance, so that some players can manipulate the game to serve their own interests. Knowledge of the game is, therefore, useful to play poker or bet on horse racing but is of very little use to purchase lottery tickets or play slot machines.

A gambler may engage in the game itself while gambling on its outcome (card games, craps), or he may be prevented from participating actively in an activity in which he has personal stakes (professional sports, lottery). Without the accompanying betting activity, some games are dull or almost meaningless and are rarely played unless wagering takes place (coin tossing, poker, dice games, lotteries). In other sports, gambling is not necessarily part of the game, and the correlation is merely traditional and not necessary for the performance of the match itself (horse racing, soccer pools). Casinos and racetracks, which are commercial establishments, may arrange to gamble when it is easy to acquire a portion of the money wagered by patrons by participating as a favorite party in the game, renting space, or withdrawing a portion of the betting pool. Some very large-scale activities (horse racing, lotteries) usually require business and professional organizations to present and maintain them effectively.

A rough estimate of the approximate amount of money lawfully wagered in the world every year is around $10 trillion (illegal gambling may even surpass that figure). Lotteries are the world's leading form of gambling in terms of total turnover. State-licensed or state-operated lotteries expanded rapidly during the late 20th century in Europe and the United States and are widely distributed worldwide. Organized soccer pools can be found in almost all European countries, most countries in South America, Australia, and a few countries in Africa and Asia. Most of these countries also provide wagering on other sporting events, whether state-organized or statelicensed.

In English-speaking countries and France, betting on horse racing is a leading form of gambling. It exists in many other countries too. Wherever horse racing is famous, it has typically become a major business with its newspapers and other publications, comprehensive statistical services, self-styled experts offering betting advice, and sophisticated communication networks providing information to betting centers, bookmakers, and their employees, and employees involved in horse care and breeding. The same applies to dog racing, although to a lesser extent. The advent of satellite broadcasting technology has resulted in the development of so-called off-track betting facilities where bettors watch live telecasts at locations away from the racetrack.

There have been casinos or gambling houses since the 17th century, at least. Gambling became ubiquitous in the 20th century and took on almost a standardized appearance all over the world. Gambling is permitted in many or most holiday resorts in Europe and South America, but not always in cities. For many years, casinos in the United States have been legal only in Nevada and New Jersey and, by exclusive license, in Puerto Rico. Still, most other states also allow casino gambling, and betting facilities operate clandestinely across the country, often through the corruption of government authorities. Roulette is one of France and Monaco's leading gambling games in casinos and is popular around the world. At most American casinos, craps are the featured dice game. Slot and video poker machines are a centerpiece of casinos in the U.S. and Europe and are also found in thousands of private clubs, restaurants, and other ventures; they are also mundane in Australia. Among the casino card games, Baccarat, in its conventional form chemin de fer, remained a major gambling game in Britain and the most frequently patronized continental casinos at Deauville, Biarritz, and the resorts of the Riviera. Faro, once the United States' largest casino game, has become obsolete. Blackjack is an American casinos' main card game. In Monte-Carlo and a few other continental casinos, the French card game trente et quarante (or rouge et noir) is played. Many other games can be played in some casinos— sic bo, fan-tan, and pai-gow poker in Asia, for example, and local games like A Boule, Banque Francesa, and Kalooki in Europe.

Poker exploded in popularity at the beginning of the 21st century, mainly through the high visibility of televised poker tournaments and the abundance of playing facilities on the Internet. Another type of Internet gambling is the so-called betting exchanges— Internet websites where players make wagers with each other, with the website taking a small cut of each wager in return for the organization and handling of the transaction.

In a broad sense of the word, stock markets can also be considered a form of betting, albeit one in which the bettors play a considerable part by making use of their skill and knowledge. This also applies to insurance; in effect, paying the premium on one's life insurance is a bet that one will die within a specific period of time. If one wins (dies), the money of insurance is paid to one's family. If one loses (survives the time specified), the insurance company holds the wager (premium), which plays the role of a bookmaker and sets the chances (payout ratios) according to actuarial statistics. Such two forms of gambling, the former gaining venture capital, and the latter distributing statistical risks are considered beneficial to society.

Problem Gambling and Gambling Addiction Gambling problems can arise from any part of life. Your gambling ranges from a casual, harmless diversion to a harmful obsession with severe consequences. Whether you're betting on sports, scratch cards, Roulette, poker, or slots
— at a casino, track, or online — a gambling issue may strain your relationships, interfere with work, and cause a financial catastrophe. You might even do stuff that you never thought you'd do, like running up huge debts or even stealing money to gamble.

Addiction to gambling is also known as pathological gambling, compulsive gambling, or gambling disorder. Thus it is an impulse-control disorder. If you're a compulsive gambler, even if it has negative consequences for you or your loved ones, you can't control the impulse to play. You're going to play whether you're up to or down, broke, or clean, and you're going to keep playing regardless of the consequences— even if you know the odds are against you or you can't afford to lose.

This book tries to unleash the myths and facts surrounding gambling while going through in detail its historical existence and how it has evolved over the years to attain its present form and types along with its widespread usage. Besides discussing various types of gambling, this book will also deliberate upon its symptoms, causes, its effects on individuals and society, and finally, ways and means to treat it successfully.

Chapter 2: Gambling And Its History

2.1 What actually is gambling?

Let us first explore the different definitions of gambling and meanings ascribed to it as an activity by various authentic wordbook sources.

Cambridge Dictionary has this definition of gambling:

The activity of taking a risk in money on the result of something, such as a game or horse race, hoping to make money.

Collins describes gambling as:

The act of <u>betting</u> <u>money</u>, for <u>example</u>, in <u>card</u> <u>games</u> or on <u>horse</u> <u>racing</u>.

Oxford dictionary gives a precise definition of gambling in the following manner:

The activity of playing games of chance for money and of betting on horses, etc.

Princeton's WordNet treats gambling as a noun describing it as:

The activity to play for support in the hope to win (which includes the chance to win a prize or payment of a price) Finally, the Business Dictionary presents more concrete and relevant description of gambling. It explicitly says:

Gambling is a special form of betting, which must result in either a gain or a loss. Gambling is not a taking of risk in the context of speculation (assumption of significant short-term risk) or an investment (acquisition of property or assets to achieve long-term capital gains). It also differs from policies that can reduce or eliminate the risk of loss, but does not provide a legitimate chance of benefit.

The overwhelming use of words such as risk, chance, and uncertainty clearly demonstrates the unpredictable nature of gambling concerning its result and thus allude to harmful and detrimental effects it can have on individuals, families, relationships, and society at large.

There has been a swift increase in the accessibility of legalized gambling in the United States and other parts of the world over the past several decades, and especially over the past 10 to 15 years. The associations between gambling patterns and health status have been extensively investigated by a few scientific studies. Existing data support the idea that certain gambling behaviors, particularly problem gambling and pathological gambling, are correlated with non-gambling health issues. Gambling is a very common illegal practice that can be considered a non-drug related behavior with an addictive-potential. In a general medical setting, the relative importance of assessing the gambling habits of patients depends in part on the associated health risks and benefits.

Are there different types of Gambling Addiction?

Gambling displays a variety of behaviors, so there are many different types of gambling addiction. When someone is addicted to gambling, deciphering, or ascertaining the addiction is not easy. The act of gambling is not confined to slot machines, cards, and casinos, contrary to popular belief. There are other available forms of gambling, such as buying a lottery ticket, entering a raffle, or making a bet with a friend.

Gambling addiction can arise when a person feels financially ruined and believes that they can only solve their problems by risking what little they have in an effort to get a large sum of money. Sadly, this almost always leads to a cycle where the gambler thinks he has to win back his losses, and the cycle continues until the person is forced to seek rehabilitation to break his habit.

Another type of addiction to gambling results in a gambler playing the games and making extremely risky bets just to experience the emotional high associated with taking huge risks that sometimes pay off. The person affected by this addiction must be willing to stop the behavior in both situations, not just to appease family and friends.

Problem Gambling and Pathological Gambling

Gambling can also be defined as placing something of value at risk in the hopes of gaining something of greater value. Wagering in casinos and lotteries, horse and dog racing, card games, and sporting events are common ways of gambling. Gambling is an extremely widespread activity, with 86 percent of the general adult population endorsing lifelong involvement in traditional forms of gambling and 52 percent of adults reporting active involvement in past-year lottery gambling.

Gambling issues can happen to anyone from any walk of life. Your gambling ranges from a fun, harmless diversion to an extreme, unhealthy obsession. Whether you're betting on sports, scratch cards, Roulette, poker, or slots — at a casino, track, or online — a gambling problem may strain your relationships, interfere with work and cause a financial catastrophe. You might even do stuff that you never thought you'd do, like running up huge debts or even stealing money to gamble.

Gambling addiction is an impulse-control disorder and is also known as pathological gambling, compulsive gambling, or gambling disorder. If you're a compulsive gambler, even if it has negative consequences for you or your loved ones, you can't control the temptation to play. You're going to play whether you're up to or down, broke, or clean, and you're going to keep playing regardless of the consequences— even if you know the odds are against you or you can't afford to lose.

Of course, without being totally out of control, you can also have a gambling problem. Any gambling activity that disrupts your life is a problem gambling. You may be suffering from a gambling issue if you are obsessed with gambling, wasting a major portion of your time and money on it, chasing losses, or gambling in spite of serious consequences in your life.

The addiction or problem with gambling is often associated with other disorders of behavior or mood.

Many problem gamblers can also suffer from substance abuse issues, unmanaged ADHD, stress, depression, anxiety, or bipolar disorder. You will also need to tackle these and any other underlying causes to resolve your gambling issues.

While most people gamble, a minority meets the criteria for a gambling disorder. Pathological gambling is the most extreme pattern of pathological or harmful gambling activity. It is the only gambling condition for which specific diagnostic criteria exist in the current American Psychiatric Association's (DSM-IV-TR) Diagnosis and Statistical Manual. In other words, problem gambling is often used to describe habits of excessive or harmful gambling that are less serious but disruptive, often inclusive, and sometimes exclusive of pathological gambling.

Pathological Gambling: An Addiction or Compulsion?

Two common, non-mutually exclusive pathological gambling conceptualizations identify the condition as an impulse control disorder located along an obsessivecompulsive spectrum or as drug addiction. Although data are available to support each categorization, broad proband trials of the obsessive-compulsive disorder have not typically reported increased rates of pathological gambling, nor have high rates of obsessive-compulsive disorder been identified in samples of the problem or pathological gamblers. The St. Louis Epidemiologic Catchment Area (ECA) study, for example, found an odds ratio of 0.6 in the problem or pathological gamblers, compared to non-gamblers, for obsessive-compulsive disorder. Compulsive traits, however, have long been defined as a core component of addiction. Current studies into the underlying neurobiologies are being undertaken to establish more accurately the correlation between "behavioral" dependency such as pathological gambling and addictions to drugs.

Gambling: Prevalence Rates

Prevalence rates of gambling activity and problem and pathological gambling have risen as a result of increasing legalized status of gambling opportunities. A metaanalysis of prevalence studies conducted over the past several decades found prevalence rates of 1.1 percent and 1.6 percent in adults, respectively, for pathological gambling and 2.8 percent and 3.8 percent for problem gambling, respectively. For primary care settings, similar or slightly higher rates were recorded (6.2 percent for one study), and consistently higher rates were found in other specific populations, including teenagers, persons in correctional facilities, and people with mental health problems.

2.2 A Brief History of Gambling

Gambling has been taking place, in some form or other, for hundreds if not thousands of years. From ancient China where traces of primitive games of chance were discovered on tiles to Egypt where the oldest known dice were digging out to scenes on Greek and Roman pottery showing that betting on animal fights was normal and animals would be bred for that sole purpose, humans love to play and do so at any opportunity.

About 200 BC' white pigeon ticket' was played in China's gambling houses with the local governor's approval, who would have earned a percentage of the profits, and the winnings were often used to finance state works; both Harvard and Yale were both initially funded by lottery money that they continue to use today.

It is believed that it was in the 9th century in China that playing cards first appeared, although the games played are unknown, and the cards have little resemblance to those used today. The cards were often adorned with human forms, but the Kings and Queens that we are more familiar with started to appear as games spread across Europe.

The Comprehensive History of Gambling

Human history is inextricably linked with gambling, as no matter how long you travel, there are indications that gambling is probably going on wherever groups of people come together. Now we're not going to try to track every single twist and turn on the evolution of gambling. However, we will select a few of the big dates to serve as benchmarks on the path to today's gaming adventure. **The Earliest Evidence of Gambling-2300bc**

Although it is almost certain that certain types of betting have been very actively followed since the start of human civilization, the earliest concrete evidence comes from ancient China where tiles were found that seemed to have been used for a rudimentary game of chance. The Chinese' Book of Songs' refers to "the drawing of wood," indicating that the tiles actually should have been a part of a lottery-type game. There is ample evidence in the form of keno slips that were used as some lottery in about 200bc to finance state works—probably including the construction of China's Great Wall. Lotteries have continued throughout history to be used for public purposes—both Harvard and Yale have been founded using lottery funds—and continue to do so to this day. **Dicing on the Streets of Old Rome-500bc**

The Greek poet Sophocles believed that dice were invented during Troy's siege by a mythological hero. While this may have somewhat questionable ground, his writings around 500bc were the first mention of dice in Greek history. We know that dice existed even earlier than this, as a pair had been unearthed from a 3000bc Egyptian tomb, but what's certain is that the ancient Greeks and Romans loved to play on all sorts of things, obviously at any given opportunity. In addition, within the ancient city of Rome, all forms of gambling—including dice games—were forbidden, and a fine levied on those caught was worth four times the bet. As a result, clever Roman people invented the first gambling chips, so they could claim to play only for chips and not for real money if they were nabbed by the guards. (Note that if you try at a Vegas casino, this ruse will not work).

Playing your Cards Right in China-800ad

Many scholars agree that in the 9th century, the first playing cards appeared in China, although the precise rules of the games for which they were used were lost in history. Many say that the tickets were both the game and the stake, such as today's children's trading card games, while other sources claim that the first packs of cards were Chinese domino paper types. The cards used at this time certainly had very little to do with the traditional 52 card decks that we know today.

Baccarat in Italy and France-1400s

The oldest game still played in casinos today is Baccarat's two-player card game, a variant of which was first mentioned when it spread from Italy to France as early as the 1400s. It took hundreds of years and various inventions to enter the game we know today, despite its early genesis. Although the game's various incarnations have come and gone, the standard version played in casinos all over the world came from Cuba to the U.S. through Britain, with a few changes to the rules along the way. While Baccarat is more of a spectator sport than a game, due to its popularity with high-rolling gamblers, it is a feature of just about every casino.

Blackjack through the Ages-.1600

Many believe the early blackjack was created out of a Spanish game named "ventiuno" (21) as the game was published by Don Quixote's writer in 1601. The inventors of chance games were seldom documented in the historical annals as they were with all these origin stories.

The Spanish game of 21 of the 17th century is undoubtedly a clear progenitor of the modern game, and this genre has entered the United States with early European settlers. The term "blackjack" was a novelty in the United States and was related in the 1930s to special promotions in Nevada casinos 10 to 1 bets have been charged to draw new buyers if the game.

First Casinos in Italy-1638

In the early 17th century in Italy began to emerge the first gaming houses which could accurately be associated with casinos. In 1638, for example, in the context of the yearly carnival, the Ridotto was built in Venice in order to ensure a safe gambling atmosphere. In the 19th century, Casinos began to emerge in continental Europe, while U.S. gambling houses were in high demand in the same period. Damp boats that carry wealthy farmers and merchants up and down the Mississippi have been the venue for many informal activities like gambling. Today, as we talk about the casino, we prefer to see the Las Vegas Strip that rose out of the remnants of the American depression.

The Little Wheel in Paris-1796

As we are already informed, Roulette was developed in the Paris gambling houses where the players knew (ironically enough) the device we now refer to as the American Roulette wheel. This took another 50 years to complete the' American' edition, and millions of roulette players could be thankful for this. Roulette became mainstream over the 19th century and, when the famed Monte Carlo casino developed the single zero-shaped design, it expanded across Europe and throughout most of the world even if the Americans stayed by the initial double-zero wheels

Poker: Bust to Boom-1829

It's hard to pinpoint the exact roots of poker as poker seems organically to have evolved from different card games in many of these competitions over the decades and perhaps centuries. Some have poker roots from Persia in the 17th century, while others claim the game we know today was influenced by a French game called Poque. What we definitely know is that Joseph Crowell's English actor recorded a familiar game style in New Orleans in 1829, so it's just dated the same as the birth of poker. The increase in demand and popularity of the game was rather slower until the 70s saw the launch of the world poker tournaments. Moreover, the emergence of online poker and T.V. events that enabled viewers to see the hands of players really exploded. Since qualifying for and winning the 2003 World Poker Championship, amateur Chris Moneymaker encouraged everyone to imagine themselves as millionaires of the online poker business.

One-Armed Bandits Appear in New York-1891

The very first gambling system that was comparable to the slots which we hear of today was one that was built by Mr. Sittman and Mr. Pitt in New York. Charles Fey in San Francisco invented the Liberty Bell machine around the same time. The system was much more realistic in that winnings could be controlled specifically and marked the start of the real slot game revolt. This dated back to this early innovation that some new video slot games still had bell signals. Whilst early machines distributed cigarettes and rubber rather than currency, cashdispensing models quickly became a standard of bars and casinos around the world, and in 1976 the first video slot was created, paving the way for the following online video slots.

Gambling in the U.S.: Two Sides of the Same Coin1910

The U.S. has always had up-and-down connections regarding gambling since the very beginning of Western colonialism. When Puritan settler movements forbade gambling in their new settlements, emigrants from England found gambling much and were more than pleased to accept it. The dichotomous connection has remained unchanged until now, and public pressure in 1910 contributed to a national ban on playing gambling. Just like the ban of alcohol at the same moment, this was somewhat difficult to implement, and the game was marginally discreet. The fall of Wall Street and the Great Depression in the early 1930s forced gambling to be allowed, as, for many, it had been the sole hope of alleviating their grinding poverty. While in many countries most popular in Las Vegas, Nevada, online gambling is legal today, however, it is still a gray area in the U.S. For now, several foreign internet casinos do not welcome American clients, but this will improve in the near future.

The New Frontier for Gambling-1994

Microgaming is among the world's largest creators of casinos and poker machines, and it is also a developer of web gambling. The leap into the world of real casinos was created in 1994, something like 2300bc on the Internet. In 5 years, online gambling amounts to over
$1 billion, and today's industry is growing and multibillion dollars with over 1000 online casinos.

In 1996 the Kahnawake Gaming Commission was set up, which controlled online gaming operations and granted gambling licenses to many of the world's online casinos and poker rooms in the Mohawk territory of Kahnawake. This is an attempt to maintain fair and transparent the activities of registered online gambling firms.

Immediately after, the Internet Gambling Prohibition Act of 1999 had been passed, indicating that no online gambling service could be offered to any U.S. citizen. That hadn't applied. Online gaming for multi-players was also launched in 1999.

Playtech came in 2003 to the first live dealer casinos and brought us closer to a fusion between brick and mortar casinos and the virtual world.

Gambling Has Gone Mobile-2019

A new generation of players has brought technological advances. Evidence shows Web users are less likely to use the desktops and are more likely to use handheld devices. The same applies to those who like online gambling and enjoy playing on the go. The biggest gambling websites acknowledged the trend in use, and smartphone gambling now provides many more options.

Mobile devices are preferred to be useful for participants; players have immediate access to wagering opportunities and gambling, and on the same mobile platforms as operators understand that social networking is engaging with each other.

There is a rapid increase in people interested in it since New Jersey allowed online gambling in 2011. America has seen a drive to legalize it by state and the rapid increase in mobile gambling

The Future

It's as hard to predict the potential for gambling, as it's to discover some of the roots of today's gambling games. However, at the moment, a lot of attention is paid to the mobile gaming industry, where online casinos struggle to make games more compliant with recent handheld devices. The development of virtual reality is only taking the first steps as a business venture and you can be confident that gaming applications will take place. How would you like to sit down with a group of friends from all over the world at a virtual poker table, share some fun, try and tell if you're going to see a facial tick from home? Revolution. V.R. Headsets will make it happen perhaps not now, but definitely in some years' time if technology keeps advancing so rapidly.

Gambling on the Blockchain

Blockchain technology and cryptocurrency are transforming the gambling industry in respects that we hadn't yet dreamed a few years ago. It is becoming commonplace for casinos to use cryptocurrency for gaming and can be used as either the principal payment system or as an alternative to fiat-based payment systems. The Blockchain provides transparency, reduces the edge of the house, and reduces transaction costs. The Blockchain enables users to play freely and almost automatically withdrawal and deposit rates, so saving documentation or even building an account does not need to be handed over.

Blockchain technology has the same ability to play, enabling everybody to be a casino player. Although certain Bitcoin casinos allow users to finance casinos and gain from household share, they have been brought to the next stage through crypto platforms such as Ethereum, where ventures have created a system where token holders have separated automatically from the income that the Blockchain produces. Some create blockchain-based gaming technologies that allow casino operators with a zero-house edge, close-to-null transaction charges, and equal random numbers to develop and implement gaming applications.

There may be likely to become more advanced in this field, with developer teams introducing new gambling possibilities using blockchain technology.

Edgefund is one notion like that; Edgefund would create a joint bankroll that will enable approved players to create games that provide very significant payouts on the Edgefund site. Game promoters may offer fixed-odds games for themselves at zero financial risks, i.e., assured income for every bet they position. To do so, Edgefund must purchase the possibility from the game developers at the lowest mathematically confirmed expense to cover the central bankroll of the Edge Fund. This means that a rival intelligent contract cannot defeat Edge Fund and that game-operators cannot ruin themselves.

And then? Alright, nobody knows, but everything is possible when it comes to gambling.

Chances, Probabilities, and Odds in Gambling

Events or occurrences that are somewhat likely to occur in each case have equal opportunities. Every instance is completely independent in pure chance games; that is, every play has the same likelihood of achieving a given outcome as each of the other. In fact, assumptions of probability refer to a long-term series of events and occasions but not to single ones. The law of higher numbers is an expression of the fact that as the number of events increases, the ratios expected by probability statements become increasingly correct, but the absolute number of outcomes of a particular form departs from expectations with increasing frequency as the number of repetitions increases. It is the percentages that are reliable correctly, not the individual events or exact figures.

Among all possibilities, the likelihood of a favorable outcome can be expressed: probability (p) is equal to the total number of favorable outcomes (f) divided by the total number of possibilities (t), or p= f / t. But this applies only in luck-ruled cases. For example, in a twodice tossing game, the final number of expected outcome is 36 (each of six sides of one die paired with each of six sides of the other) and the number of ways of creating, say, seven is six (made by tossing 01 and 06, 02 and 05, 03 and 04, 04 and 03, 05 and 02, or 06 and 01); thus, the likelihood of throwing a seven is 6/36 or 1/6.

It is common to represent the concept of possibility in terms of odds toward winning in most gambling games. This is actually the ratio of the desirable to the unfavorable possibilities. Because the possibility of throwing a seven is 1/6, on average, one in six throws would be advantageous, and five would not; thus, the chances of throwing a seven are 5 to 1. The possibility of getting heads in a coin toss is 1/2; the chances are one to one, sometimes called. Care must be taken to understand the expression on average, which most correctly refers to a greater number of cases and is not useful in individual cases. A common fallacy of gamblers called the maturity theory of chances (or the fallacy of Monte-Carlo), wrongly assumes that each game in a game of chance depends on the others and that a sequence of outcomes of one kind should be balanced by the other possibilities in the short run. Gamblers have developed a number of systems largely on the basis of this mistake; casino operators are delighted to promote the use of such systems and exploit the lack of the strict rules of chance and independent play by any gambler. Nevertheless, an interesting example of a game where each game relies on previous games is blackjack, where cards already used to deal from the dealing shoe influence the composition of the remaining cards; for example, if all the aces (value 1 or 11 points) were dealt, a "real" (a 21 with two cards) can no longer be accomplished. This assumption forms the basis for certain schemes where the house advantage can be overcome.

In some games, the dealer, the banker (the person collecting and redistributing the stakes), or some other player may have an advantage. Not all players, therefore, have equal chances of winning or equal payoffs. This inequality can be rectified by alternating between the players in the game positions. Nonetheless, commercial gambling operators typically make their

profits by consistently holding an advantaged role as the dealer, or they charge money for the opportunity to play or deduct a proportion of the wagers on each game. In the dice game of craps— one of the big casino games providing the most favorable odds to the gambler— the casino returns to winners from 3/5 of 1 percent to 27 percent lower than the equal odds, depending on the type of bet made. Depending on the bet, the house advantage ("vigorous") for Roulette in American casinos ranges from about 5.26 to 7.89 percent and varies from
1.35 to 2.7 percent in European casinos. In the long run, the house always has to prevail. Some casinos also add rules that improve their earnings, especially rules that limit the sums that may be staked under certain circumstances.

Most gambling games contain, as well as chance, elements of physical ability or strategy. Like most other card games, the game of poker is a mixture of chance and strategy that also involves a great deal of psychology. Making a bet on horse racing or athletic contests involves evaluating the physical capacity of a contestant and using other assessment skills. For those gamblers who are sponsored by very few dealers and small if the players are assisted by a relatively large number of bettors, In order to ensure that chance plays a major role to decide the results of such activities, weights, disabilities or other corrective measures may be implemented in certain situations to give the players approximately equal opportunities to win, and changes should be made in the payoffs so that the probability of success and the severity of the payoffs are put in opposite proportion to each, For example, pari-mutuel pools in horse-race betting reflect different horses ' chances of winning as players anticipate. , the greater the option, the lower the individual payout. The same applies to bet on sports events with bookmakers (illegal in most of the U.S. but legal in England). Bookmakers typically take bets on the result of what is perceived to be an unequal match by allowing the side to be more likely to win to score more than a simple majority of points; this practice is known as setting a "point spread." For example, in a game of American or Canadian football, the more respected team would have to win, say, by more than 10 points. Give it is backing an even payout.

Sadly, in most gambling games, such processes can be interfered with to preserve the power of chance; cheating is possible and relatively straightforward. Much of the stress associated with gambling has been caused by some of its promoters and players ' dishonesty, and a large proportion of current gambling law is written for cheating regulation. Nevertheless, more regulations were tailored to governments ' attempts to extract tax revenue from gambling than to prevent cheating.

2.3 Types of Gambling

Gambling games can be classified into two groups, games dependent on chance, and games based on skills. Note, while luck plays a bigger role in games based on opportunity, it is an important force in games based on skill. For 100 percent accuracy, 100 percent of the time, game outcomes can never be expected in all types of legal gaming.

- Chance-based (100% contingent on chance)

- Skill-based (players have some control, but the chance remains an outcome factor)

Chance Based Gambling

Participants have no ability to change or influence the result of chance-based gambling, which is entirely dependent on random events.

**Games /
Activities: Casino
games:**
- Slot machines

- Progressive bonuses

- Bingo

- Roulette

- Sic Bo

- Baccarat

- Lottery products:

- 50/50 raffles

- Pull-tabs

- Scratch'n win tickets

- 6/49

- BC/49

- Lotto Max

- Keno

- Pacific Hold 'em

Slot machine gambling is one of the most common forms of gambling dependent on chance. Game results are unpredictable in chance-based gambling games and are based entirely on random events. Teams have no way of influencing or impacting how the game ends and whether they win or lose their bet.

Chance-based gamblers may get into trouble, so they overestimate their degree of control over the game outcome. Most players are naming it opportunity. A person that knows they are fortunate or feels lucky will make decisions that they would not normally make when playing. It is crucial for chance-based gamblers to have a good understanding of how gambling actually functions, and to be mindful of prudent gambling techniques in order to keep gambling healthy and enjoyable.

Examples of Chance-Based Gambling

Casino and Community Gaming Center Games and Sports Slot machines Modern Bingo and Most table games (Roulette, sic bo, Baccarat, etc.) The pace or order of bets does not affect outcomes, nor does the player, venue, or table or system past, since each game is separate and random.

Lottery Products

- 50/50 raffles

- Pull-tabs

- Scratch'n win tickets

These products often provide set prizes that must be won individually.

Other Lottery Products

- 6/49

- BC/49

- Lotto Max

- Keno

- Pacific Hold 'em

Such lottery items can have awards split with multiple winners without winners or prizes. Prices can be fixed in advance or can be decided by selling tickets.

There are many types, locations, modes, and representations of gambling dependent on chance, but they all have one thing in common: all players have an equal chance of winning at all moments.

It is common to use the term ' chance' to apply to' likelihood' as in' what is the possibility that it will rain today? Luck' is often associated with' odds," randomness' and' probability.'

Skill-Based Gambling

In skill-based gambling, players can use betting strategies and techniques based on related knowledge or other players' decisions and behavior.

Games / Activities

Strategy, skill, knowledge, and chance

- Poker

- Blackjack

- Pai Gow

- Texas Shootout

- Horse Race Betting

- Sports Betting

Poker is the most popular type of skill-based gaming, where players compete with each other rather than the dealer in the room. Players benefit from prior experience playing the game in skill-based games. Techniques and tactics can be used, and some playing styles can be effective when playing the exact similar players more than once.

Nevertheless, it is important to remember that skillbased gambling is still gambling, so the outcome of the game is largely beyond the influence of each participant.

Poker players will overestimate their skill level and underestimate their opponents ' skill level. Players also get into trouble by misjudging the degree of control they have over the result of the game, as they have no power over what cards they are issued, what cards they are dealt with their opponents, and what choices their opponents may make.

Due to the unexpected outcome in all forms of gambling, particularly skill-based gambling, it is important to warn players about prudent gambling techniques in order to ensure that gambling remains a safe and fun game.

Examples of Skill Based Gambling

- Race and Sports Betting Activities

- Horse Race Betting

- Sports Betting

- Players use their experience for placing their bet on sport, celebrities, animals, etc.

For example, once a gamble is made, it is not necessary to affect the outcome, and it becomes the outcome of chance. For a fact, other bettors and bookmakers (bookmakers) use the same expertise to assess the payoff odds.

Casino Games / Activities
- Poker

- Blackjack

- Pai Gow

- Texas Shootout

Players can use betting strategies and techniques to try winning a hand or getting an advantage. Such tactics and methods may be focused on the behavior and action of other players for poker.

Strategies and tactics make it possible to monitor more participants than in mere chance games, but the consequences of wagers remain unpredictable. While strategies and techniques can help, there is no scheme that can be used to win every hand or eliminate the advantage of the house.

Chapter 3: Gambling: Myths. Psychology and Facts

No other practice associated with it has as many misconceptions as gambling. The volume of formally and informally spread misinformation is overwhelming. However, it has something to do with the luck-gambling relationship.

Superstitious people in a way that logical people don't believe in things this leads to the belief that there are many falsehoods that can devastate your bankroll.

Most of the public playing games often dislike math. Since gambling and luck are closely related, it should not shock anyone that gambling myths are similar to some basic math concepts.

Some Compulsive Gambling Myths and Facts Most people involved in recreational gambling don't think they might ever become addicted. After all, they only occasionally engage in gambling, never lose in one sitting more than a few hundred dollars, and always act responsibly.

Some people may not realize that until it's too late, their gambling habit has become an addiction. Here are some compulsive gambling myths that might surprise you.

Myth: Every day, compulsive gamblers are playing.

Fact: How often a person plays does not have a gambling addiction relationship. Pathological gamblers are only allowed to play once a week or once a month. It's the gambler's behaviors ' emotional and financial effects that signify an addiction.

Myth: When you lose every last penny, gambling becomes a problem.

Fact: A gambling addiction does not decide how much money you win or lose. Gamblers can win big and then lose all their earnings the next day, or they can gamble only a certain amount each time. Usually, gamblers will incur ample debt to start affecting their lives with the financial consequences of their actions, but this is not always the case.

Myth: Something like gambling can't get addicted.

Fact: Some activities are just as addictive as drinking or doing drugs, such as gambling. Gambling may create a euphoria that causes the player to continue to replicate the behavior in order to maintain this result. The gambler develops a desire for gambling, as with drugs and alcohol, and will take greater and greater risks to achieve this euphoria. A gambler can give into a gambling addiction by doing it more often, regardless of the negative consequences. Pathological gamblers, like any other addictions and compulsive behaviors, may also dispute their habits and may not believe they have trouble at all.

Myth: Compulsive gambling is merely a financial issue.

Fact: According to the National Council, compulsive gambling is an emotional problem with financial consequences. Even if the financial obligations of a gambler are taken care of, that person remains a compulsive gambler. The issue is not how much money the gambler has lost, but that the individual has an uncontrollable gambling addiction.

Myth: Even reckless people are gambling addicts.

Fact: It is common for people to assume that addicted people are weak-willed and reckless. But, no matter how responsible they are, anyone can become addicted to gambling. Once in their addiction, gamblers may indulge in risky activities to sustain their addiction.

Myth: The criminal behavior of all gamblers

Fact: Although some players may engage in criminal behavior, such as robbery or assault, this is not the norm. Often it's a sense of loss of control that drives a player to engage in such behaviors.

Myth: A gambler is going to bet on anything.

Fact: Gamblers usually prefer what they're going to be on and won't be tempted by betting on other issues. For example, lottery tickets or slot machines may not tempt a gambler who makes weekly trips to the race track.

Myth: If the gambler can afford it, compulsive gambling is not really a problem.

Fact: Just because people lose money doesn't mean their actions aren't problematic. Compulsive gambling usually interferes with all facets of the gambler's life, including family and friends and work relationships. The concern is the gambling conduct itself, not the financial effects of the crime.

Myth: This means paying off all their debts to help compulsive gamblers break their addiction.

Fact: The persistent bailing out of debt of a compulsive gambler can only make the conduct probable. Although getting the debt repaid may be a priority, treating the gambling addiction itself and getting the help needed to overcome the addiction is more important to the gambler.

Myth: A compulsive gambler is easy to recognize.

Fact: Unlike drug and alcohol addictions, there are very few obvious signs of compulsive gambling. The behavior is easy to hide from people, particularly if they are addicted to gambling.

If any of these myths are realities for you or a loved one, gambling addiction may need to be treated.

Many of the words that we use have origins in gambling. Think about how many times a day you start a phrase, "I bet..." Here are a few more examples:

The chances are

- It's a sure thing!
- It's a crapshoot.
- I've got an ace in the hole

It's a safe bet (another term from gambling) that you've used such phrases before! All these common words prove that gambling has been around for a long time— long enough to build a few myths. Here are a few other common gambling myths and facts.

Myth: Gambling is a means of making money.

Fact: Gambling is a way to lose money more often than not. If you're playing, think of it as something you've got to pay for, just like a movie or dinner with friends. That can help you keep playing in perspective— and if you end up winning any money now and then, it's going to be a nice treat instead of relying on something you've been.

Myth: People will tell if heads or tails of a coin toss would come up.

Fact: Each coin flip is a separate event. What happened in the previous flips doesn't matter. The probability of a single flip of heads or tails is 50 percent, regardless of how many times you turn the coin.

Myth: There are mechanisms that make winning lottery numbers easier to predict.

Fact: How you choose the numbers doesn't matter; your chances of winning are always the same. Take, for example, a lottery-like Lotto 6/49. All the numbers are mounted in a drum and mixed together. By chance, the range is perfect. The number has the same probability of being chosen (a 1 in 49 chance of being accurate). For one ticket, the odds of winning the jackpot are 1 in 13,983,816.

Myth: The majority of teenagers are not playing.

Fact: gambling for about 2 out of 3 teenagers

Myth: Teens are not having issues with gambling.

Fact: Teens tend to play with friends, not in casinos, but that doesn't mean that they can't have gambling issues. A 2008 study of Alberta students in grades 7 to 12 found signs of problem gambling, just over 2 percent, so about 2 out of every 100 students surveyed. Approximately 4 percent or 4 out of 100 students showed signs of risk of developing gambling problems.

Myth: When they have a losing streak, people can usually win back their money.

Fact: Not true, not true! Casinos remain in business because most people don't get back their money. Think about it: how long would a casino remain in business if it spent more money than it took in? The truth is that in these places, most gamblers lose much more money than they win.

Myth: Lottery winning will put you on "easy street."

Fact: You're not under the age of 18! In Alberta, purchasing lottery tickets, collecting lottery winnings, or playing any other game sponsored by the Alberta Gaming and Liquor Commission is against provincial lottery regulations for those under 18. (Including scratch-andwin tickets.) Some Pervasive Myths & Facts Myth: The more you're playing, the more likely you're going to have a big win.

Fact: Any gambling event's result is due to chance. Spending longer gambling has no impact on the outcome of the next game. This is known as the' event independence'-each outcome of an event (e.g., lottery draw or reel spin) is independent of those before or after. Given the edge of the house and return to the mechanics of the player mentioned above, a longer amount of time spent playing games would usually mean paying more for that leisure time.

Myth: You'll eventually win all of your money back if you keep playing for long enough.

Fact: The more you're playing, the more likely you're going to lose more money. The odds are always in favor of those offering the bet–the bookies, casinos and lottery companies know that some people are going to win, but more people are going to have to lose in order to keep the companies in the business.

Myth: A good knowledge of a game improves the chances of winning.

Fact: It's all down to chance, once again. Games like poker and sports betting can take advantage of extra knowledge, but you can't guess the outcome. You may think you're the best poker player in the world, but somebody else might be better or have stronger cards. The last two matches may have won your football team, but that doesn't mean they're going to win a third. Remember to play it safe at all times.

Myth: Keeping track of previous results when playing games can help you figure out the results to come.

Fact: When it comes to gambling, there is no pattern. If a pattern existed, it would all learn, and no one would ever lose. If no one was lost, there would be no money left in the slot machines, and the bookies and casinos would be bankrupt, and the winners could not be paid. Believing this will only make you lose a lot of cash and stop playing fun.

Myth: I've almost won; I've got to have a victory.

Fact: Winning "nearly" doesn't mean there's a real win around the corner. Future results of gambling are not influenced by previous results in any way.

Myth: I'm going to increase my chances of winning if I play more than one slot machine or in more than one poker game at a time.

Fact: Of course, by playing two slot machines or poker games at a time, you can win more often, but make no mistake about it: you'll also spend — and ultimately lose
— more on it. Note, the more you play, the more you lose.

Myth: If I see a certain card regularly coming up in a poker game, I will bet on it because it's likely to come up again very soon.

Fact: In a 52-card deck, 2.6 million hands are possible. As each hand is independent of the last, there is no more (or less) probability that one card will come up again once it has already appeared than any other card.

Myth: I've got a special strategy to help me succeed. I pick a lottery number and press the stop button on a slot machine at the right time.

Fact: The outcome of most chance games, particularly lotteries and slot machines, is completely random: no matter what you do, you cannot influence it. It means that betting the same numbers each week will not help you win more than betting different numbers. For example, the odds of winning Lotto 6/49 are 1 in 14 million each time you play: no matter how many people have purchased tickets or how many numbers you play, the odds are the same, regardless.

Whether you win or not playing slot machines is based solely on the randomly drawn numbers created by the computer of the machine — numbers that decide the outcome of the game even before the reels stop. When you figure out what the outcome of the game is, pressing the stop button will speed up, but it won't affect what that outcome is in any way.

Myth: I feel like it's my lucky day today. I feel that I'm going to win.

Fact: The expectation, urge, or even need to win money has no effect whatsoever on the outcome of a chance game. The FacebookMore1 Myth: Gambling is not addictive.

Fact: The idea behind the misconception that gambling is not really addictive argues that gambling has no physical effect, such as alcohol and drugs. But that's not really valid–because you believe your body has nothing to do with the brain.

The U.S. has an awful record of mental illness identification. Because the way cancer or heart disease does not always come with physical symptoms, people think that mental sickness is somehow less of a disease than a physical illness.

This kind of backward thinking destroys lives and interferes with the chances that people have to get well. Not every player gets addicted.

But it does not help anyone to say that gambling is really addictive.

Myth: You'll finally have to change your luck, and you'll start to win.

Fact: This is an example of the gambler's mistake of a mathematical concept. The theory is that past results will affect future outcomes somehow.

This is not true with most (not all) gambling activities.

Here's an example: somebody playing roulette sees the result is black four times in a row. She could make 1 of 2 hypotheses:

Black is hot and on the next spin is more likely to come up again.

Red is due, and the next spin is more likely to occur.

But the likelihood of getting a black or red result depends on how many red results there are relative to how many black outcomes there are.

Since there are still all 38 of the pockets on a roulette wheel–they don't go anywhere when you reach them—the likelihood has not changed.

That roulette wheel spin is a separate event. Previous outcomes will not affect future outcomes.

Blackjack is an exception because the deck's composition is different once a card is dealt with.

Myth: When you go to be lucky, you're psychic, and you learn.

Fact: The outcomes of gambling are randomly decided. No one has any form of supernatural ability to improve their chances of winning at casino games. But many people believe they know when they will be fortunate.

Trying to convince someone who thinks he's psychic that he can't predict the future is probably pointless. Though, if it were not included, it wouldn't be a good list of gambling myths.

Spend some time reading about James Randi, who has spent decades debunking psychics, to find out more about why paranormal phenomena are a bunch of hokum. His foundation has been offering $1 million to anyone who could demonstrate documented paranormal activity for over 50 years–particularly psychological ability.

No one ever participated, and over 1,000 people took part in the contest in a few years.

Myth: Casinos are pumping oxygen to keep you alive and playing games in the sun.

Fact: You should be told by some common sense that this is not valid. For a minute, think about it. When interacting with air, what is the greatest danger?

This makes things more flame-retardant.

It would be a fire hazard like no other to pump oxygen into a crowded casino with its heavy use of electricity and its large number of people who often smoke cigarettes.

The theory is probably derived from a book by Mario Puzo, Fools Die, in which a fictional casino called Xanadu pumped in oxygen. The problem is its fiction.

At The Hoaxes Museum, you can learn more about this story.

Myth: Count Cards are illegal.

Fact: A little thought clarifies the fallacy of this theory. How could thinking about a game while you're playing it be illegal? Unless you use some kind of tool to keep up with the count, all you do is worry about the game you're playing when you're counting cards.

By the way, casinos are all right with this story. We discourage the easiest way to count cards. They're actually going to take countermeasures if they think you're counting cards. On each hand, they could start shuffling the deck. Or they might ask you not to play blackjack games. If they're really sticklers, they could even permanently ban you from their casino.

But for counting cards, you cannot be charged or punished. It is not illegal.

Myth: Are Rigged Casino Games.

Fact: This theory is valid in a sense, but not the way most people think.

Those who are persuaded that casino games are rigged claim that the casino will change the game results arbitrarily whenever they feel like it.

Remember the Casablanca scene where Rick asks the croupier to land the ball on some result?

This is fiction.

That's not happening in real life. Imagine the chances of landing a roulette ball at will in one of 38 pockets.

This makes no sense.

Nevertheless, casino games are designed with math that benefits the player's casino. A gambler can win in the short run, but it is less likely than losing.

The casino is always going to win over the player in the long run.

This is because, at lower odds, the bets pay off than the odds of winning.

In our post about the house edge and how it works, you can learn more about this idea.

The math behind the edge of the house is why casinos need not rig their games. The math is rigged already.

Myth: Illegal online gaming

Fact: Too universal to be valid is this assertion. Applying to a whole country like the United States is even too common. The U.S. laws are a patchwork of federal, state, and local governments–each also has different rules.

In fact, online casino gambling has been legalized by three states in the US. The other 47 states have not legalized or regulated online casinos, but not all of them have book laws that specifically make the activity illegal.

Facilitating money transfers for illegal gambling purposes is illegal, but this is another practice from placing a bet.

And while online gambling is clearly illegal in many states in the United States, no one has ever been arrested or prosecuted on the Internet for playing slot machines or blackjack. Until now, enforcement efforts have concentrated on online gambling companies rather than players.

Myth: It's all joy.

Fact: Luck plays a part in gambling, but not necessarily in your way of thinking. A mathematician would think that luck in your expected results is just a short-term fluctuation. In the long run, things are even going to come out.

But the belief that the outcomes of gambling are based entirely on chance ignores the role that good decisionmaking plays in gambling winning.

Here's an example: Blackjack is a game wherein the math behind the game, your decisions play a clear role. Each way a hand is played has an expected value. Your job as a player is to select the highest expected value for the decision. You're playing with basic strategy when you do this on every possible stick.

The difference among a blackjack player who uses basic plan and one who only plays her hunches is the difference between 0.5% and 4% house edge.

What does your bankroll mean?

When you play for $50 a hand and get 60 hands an hour, you bring $3000 into practice every hour.

You're looking for a loss of $15 per hour if you expect to lose 0.5 percent of that action. That's casino entertainment that's relatively cheap.

But if you expect to lose 4 percent of that action, you see a $120 per hour loss. This is a relatively expensive casino entertainment.

So common sense tells you that if the bottom of the house is lower, the chances of going away from a winner are greater.

Myth: To get an advantage on your next bet, you can use patterns.

Fact: This theory is closely connected with the fallacy of the gamblers above. Here's how the thinking works: at a Jacks or Better video poker machine, you're watching a play. You see, he's only played for 2 hours, but twice he's already hit a royal flush.

You believe that the pattern is to pay jackpots more often than other games for that console.

That's not real, though.

On a Jacks or Better video poker game, the odds of winning a jackpot are still about 40,000 to 1. The previous results do not change the number of cards in the deck or the variations that you will see on your computer.

Trends are taking place in gambling games. They really happen all the time.

But in retrospect, they are only apparent.

Depending on a pattern you've seen in the past, you can't predict what will happen in the future.

Myth: Cold and/or hot slot machines.

Fact: This is closely linked to the patterns and gamblers' fallacy bullet points. Die lovers of hard slot machines won't believe this, but retrospectively slot machines only get hot or cold. Just because a game of slots has been running hot for an hour or two does not mean that it will continue to run shot in the future. It also doesn't mean that "being cold" is more likely.

Modern slot machines are operated by a random number generator (RNG) computer program. This is a computer program that produces numbers per second at a rate of thousands of numbers. If you push the "turn" button or pull the lever, at that millisecond, the RNG will stop at whatever number it counted.

This computer program is not working slowly enough to allow you to predict where it is in its count. There is no way to know if the game paid off a lot or not.

Every reel spin is a separate event. The outcomes of subsequent spins are not influenced by previous spins.

Myth: The choices made by other blackjack players influence your winning chances.

Fact: This is one of the blackjack's most common myths. It has several permutations.

Another example is the assumption that the odds are ruined by a player jumping in and out of games. There is anecdotal evidence from many players that things went well at the table until a certain player arrived. Then there is a boom! The dealer wins the whole time.

This is an example of selective memory that is better than most people realize. Just because something happens before something else doesn't mean there's a connection between cause and effect. Probably most people forget someone jumped into a game all the time and all the players started winning.

The more popular permutation is the assumption that everybody at the table is harmed by a player using a less than optimal strategy. She would take a coin, for example, that would have broken the table.

In fact, the other players at the table profit from their mistakes as often as they damage them. In the long run, it all grows.

In reality, bad players enable better blackjack games to be offered by casinos. If everyone using perfect basic strategy, casinos would change the conditions of the game to improve the players ' edge.

Myth: Gambling online is a threat to children.

Fact: Many spurious arguments against online gambling will be seen. One of these is that it places children at risk.

The fact is that most online casinos will not allow you to start playing games for real money until you have proven you are legally old enough to play. This may be 18 years old or 21 years old, depending on the casino and its jurisdiction.

Yet online casino stories that victimize kid's gamblers are unheard of.

Online gambling firms create a lot of money without targeting underage gamblers. Worldwide jurisdictions require that minors be protected from gambling as a precondition for obtaining an operating license.

Myth: Online casinos are used only for money laundering.

Fact: This is a fallacy promulgated by the UIGEA (Unlawful Internet Gambling Enforcement Act) supporters. This is a statute added in an attempt to curb offshore gaming to the Safe Ports Act.

Is there money laundering in online casinos? Maybe!
But the way to launder money is easier and safer.

Money laundering usually works by using a predominantly cash-operating business. Paper trails are anathema to a money-laundering operation, like those provided by the use of credit cards and online wallets.

I have never seen any evidence that money is being laundered by online gambling companies.

Myth: The Loosest Slot Machines Are Near the Aisles.

Fact: This theory might have been accurate at one time. The idea is that casinos want to attract gamblers to play the slots. By bringing the loosest machines closer to the aisles where people walk, they're more likely to attract gamblers to the machines.

John Robison from American Casino Guide has explored these hypotheses with casino owners and slots operators. His inference from those discussions is that the changing nature of casinos and slot machines make it unnecessary to organize slot machines in this way.

The reality is that it is not possible to find slot machines with bigger payback percentages. Even though, if you do, you also need to compensate for variables like uncertainty and win duration. A progressive slot machine with a massive jackpot might have a high potential return, but the odds of winning the big jackpot–which makes up a healthy percentage of that return–are still astronomical.

Myth: It's Impossible to Beat the Casino in the Long Run.

Fact: Most of the myths listed the point at misconceptions linked to beating the casinos.

But few people are convinced that it is not possible to beat the casino in the long run.

And that's just not real.

Many games are mathematically unbeatable. These include games like slots and roulette.

Other games are beatable by seasoned advantage gamblers, such as video poker and blackjack.

Different techniques will allow a player to gain a statistical advantage over the house, ensuring that the player can beat the casino in the long run. Counting blackjack cards is just one example of a method of advantage gambling. It's another thing to combine video poker pay tables expertise with great strategy and rebates.

Of course, by just getting lucky and stopping gambling while you're ahead, it's also possible to beat the casino in the long run.

But where is that fun?

Myth: Playing with your inserted slots club impacts your winning chances.

Fact: I explained how a random number generator works in a slot machine in an earlier bullet point. This computer program is not linked to your club card slots.

If you think about it, you will know that there is no reason for the casino to penalize players for using their club card slots. The whole point is by giving them incentives to encourage gamblers to play more.

Why are you trying to do the opposite?

The only thing that plays with your inserted slots club is to track how much money you run through the machine. The more time you spend on a slot machine and the more spins you make, the more lucrative it will be for the casino.

Casinos don't mind winners on the slot machine from time to time. The occasional wins behind the machine are already factored into the math.

The only goal of the casinos is to allow you to spend more time playing when it comes to slot machines and slot memberships.

Myth: The Casino can beat the Martingale System.

Fact: This one has some truth. Using the Martingale Method, you can often earn small wins in the short run. The concern is that a huge loss would eventually wipe out these small wins.

Here's how the Martingale Model works in theory: you bet again each time you lose a bet, doubling your bet size.

You will eventually win, recover your losses, and end up with a one-unit profit.

Here's an example: at the roulette table, a Martingale player bets on black. He's betting and losing $20. He's betting $40 on the next spin and losing again. He bets $80 on the third spin and loses. He's won back the $50 he lost on the previous two spins, and for his efforts, he's got $20 income.

The Martingale Model has two big problems: it assumes you have an infinite bankroll.

It's saying you can bet as much as you like.

In fact, you have to bet with a finite amount of money.

And even if you have a huge bankroll, you will eventually hit a winning streak where the next bet is more than the table's betting limits.

Here is an example of a Martingale progression: $20 $40 $80 $160 $320 $640 If you're betting at a table with a $500 max bet, you're only going to have to lose five times in a row before you can't keep going.

And you've lost $620 at that point.

You also lose $640 by the 6th bet to get a net profit of just $20.

Yes, the loss of 5 or 6 bets in a row is unlikely. But as you might imagine, it's not as unlikely.

Myth: On a slot machine, pulling the lever is more likely to produce a win than clicking the button "Spin."

Fact: I discussed how the random number generator on a slot machine functions in the post a few times, but for more clarification: the random number generator doesn't know whether you pulled the lever or pressed the "spin" button.

It lands on the number when you hit the button or pull the lever that you are talking about.

Moreover, what reason for such a discrepancy would the casino have?

That one just doesn't make sense. It's plain and simple superstition.

Myth: Casinos can adjust the results of the game if you have won too much.

Fact: Casinos need not adjust the outcomes of their games. All of their games already come with an integrated edge of mathematical houses that cannot beat in the long run. This is similar to the myth that a roulette wheel spin results can be controlled by the croupier.

Sometimes players win in the short run because that's the nature of likelihood. There is likely to be short-term volatility.

Casinos, on the other hand, deal almost instantly with long-term figures.

An average player is making 600 spins in an hour on a slot machine. Even if she plays four hours a day, only 2400 spins have been generated, which is statistically insignificant.

But a casino with 1000 slot machines running 24 hours a day may see 24,000 X 600 spins, or 14.4 million spins a day. Even though those games are empty 50 percent of the time on average, that's still 7 million spins a day.

Once you reach the millions of spins, you will begin to see outcomes that are close to statistical standards.

Multiply the number of spins by 30 days a month or 365 days a year, and you can easily see how the long-term casino is operating.

Because the math behind these slots games ensures a 4 percent or more long-term winnings expectation, the casino stands to make plenty of money without ever having to worry about fixing the results on their games.

The same method of thinking also applies to other casino games.

For individual players, casinos simply don't need to micromanage the results of individual games.

Myth: Bookmakers once they occur, they know the results of events.

Fact: In this post, I haven't delved into too many sports betting myths, because I'm more of casino games and poker expert.

But it's too easy to debunk this theory.

When bookmakers knew before they occurred the consequences of each case, they would be far more successful than they are. They would not have to change the lines, either, depending on the behavior of the public. They would just be sending out the lines and odds to maximize their benefit.

Bookmaking is the only way to think about it as a market, like the stock market. Based on how attractive they are for betters, lines and odds are adjusted. If a game has too much action on one side, the bookmakers will adjust their lines to try to even out the action on both sides.

They wouldn't have to do that if they knew the outcome beforehand. They would just make sure on the opposite side of the assured winner they had as much action as possible.

When determining the point spread, bookmakers are remarkably accurate. The upsets happen every week, though.

Even the Cleveland Browns win a game of football from time to time.

Myth: tickets from BC/49 are more likely to win than tickets from Lotto 6/49 because fewer people are playing because they are only available in BC.

Fact: The Lotto 6/49 winning chances are based on possible combinations of numbers, not the number of tickets sold. The matching odds of 6/6 numbers are 1 in 13,983,816. Similarly, the odds of winning BC/49 are based on possible combinations of numbers and are exactly the same as Lotto 6/49: one in 13,983,816.

Myth: "I feel lucky." or "My lucky charm will help me win."

Fact: I can't use luck to predict what's going to happen in the future. When people believe in luck, they will realize that the most common luck faced by gamblers is bad luck when it comes to gambling. Gambling outcomes are unpredictable, and gambling is risky behavior.

Myth: For a big jackpot, some slot machines are hot.

Fact: BC slots pay 92 percent of all wagered money on average. Nevertheless, the payout rate is based on a machine's life, not on one session of play. The laws of probability would encourage many players to win and cause many more to lose over the life of a slot machine or put another way, after millions and millions of spins. The truth is that slot machines have Random Number Generators (RNGs) inside them to ensure that a random result is generated by each spin. A computer is as likely to have winning combinations and big payouts back- toback as it is to have losing combinations and defeats back-to-back.

Myth: "I will learn a system that will overcome the odds."

Fact: there is no system that you can use to overcome the advantage or odds of the house. In reality, many such systems are designed to enable gamblers to bet more money than they should otherwise because they create a false sense of the potential ability of the gambler to win using the program. Many such devices that are sold to gamblers are simply designed to encourage gamblers to play even more money– allowing the player to lose more money more quickly. Each game has a random element that cannot be overcome. This is a requisite gambling condition.

Myth: "I win more at slots because I'm playing the Max Bet!"

Fact: it's true that for many slot machines if the wager made before the spin was the highest permissible (or greater than the lowest), the big win payout at better odds. Nonetheless, the average player return (ARP) still in the region of 92 percent. And essentially, when you encounter big wins, you just notice the difference, which doesn't happen very often. While you pay more to play, which increases the pace, you lose your money.

Myth: "The more I practice, the better I get."

Fact: Training is not optimal with gambling. One play doesn't affect another, and there's no system or way of winning. Note, every game has an element of chance that even with practice can't be overcome. Playing poker or betting on sports can take some skill, but these games still involve chance. You're more likely to lose over time than to win.

Myth: "Gambling.net pages are harmless and fun since there is no bet on money."

Fact: While it is true that.net sites do not require you to play money, it is important to understand that they are designed specifically to guide you to.com (pay) sites.

Practice (.net) sites make it easier for you to succeed, contributing to a false sense of competence and power.

It makes the.net pages especially dangerous for children and young people. When false assumptions are formed about one's chances, skills, or ability to win at gambling, they are difficult to overcome. False beliefs can lead to bad gambling habits and bad decision-making.

Myth: "I'm great at computer games, so I'm sure I'm going to be good at internet poker." Reality: gambling is risk-based and chance-based. The skill involved in video games has nothing to do with any kind of gambling.

Even a gambling-based video game is unlikely to have the same chances and rewards in the real world that a player will face.

Myth: "I'm going to beat everyone at bingo because I'm playing multiple cards!" Fact: with the number of cards a person plays, the chances of winning in bingo are growing, but so are the costs of playing. Most people accept this additional cost because they feel it is a significant advantage to do so. The real benefit of playing multiple bingo cards is less than expected.

Say, for instance, there are 100 cards in play. If you play five bingo cards instead of a single card, your odds go from 1-in-100 to 5-in-100. Note, though, the cost of playing has also risen five times, so you're investing your betting money five times faster, and in each bingo round, you're still likely to lose 95 out of 100 times.

The reality is that, no matter how many cards you play, the house advantage remains constant.

Myth: The problem of gambling does not affectchildren.

Fact: Research shows that about 10% to 15% of American and Canadian adolescents have encountered gambling-related issues and 1% to 6% of those individuals that meet diagnostic criteria for pathological gambling. In fact, it has been shown that children from problem gamblers are at a higher risk of developing health-related habits. It includes drug and alcohol use, gambling problems, eating disorders, depression, and suicide.

Myth: Problem gamblers ' partners often drive problem gamblers to play games.

Fact: Problem gamblers are able to find ways to streamline their gambling. Blaming others is a way to avoid taking responsibility for actions, even steps necessary to overcome the issue of gambling.

Myth: Financial issues are the main reason why the relationships of problem gamblers break down.

 Fact: It's true that money issues play a major role in ending marriages, but many non-gambling partners claim that the biggest cause is lies and lack of trust.

Myth: Problem gamblers ' parents are to blame for the actions of their children.

Fact: Most issue gamblers ' parents feel hurt and bad about the gambling actions of their son or daughter, and they are not to accept responsibility.

Myth: If a problem gambler creates a debt, the important thing to do is to help them get out as soon as possible of the financial problem.

Fact: Quick fix strategies are often appealing to everyone engaged and may seem the right thing to do, since "bailing" the gambler out of debt can actually make things worse by allowing gambling issues to continue.

Myth: It's easy to recognize problem gambling.

Fact: Secret addiction was called problem gambling. It's very easy to hide because, unlike alcohol and drug use, it has little noticeable effects. Most problem gamblers do not know that they have a problem with gambling. Problem gamblers also devote themselves to self-denial.

Chances, Myths, and Evidence

What are your chances? The odds are against you!

Do you know about the odds are of actually winning if you play for the chance to win money? The odds against the gambler are clearly stacked–that is, you should always expect to lose.

The odds are against the player in each betting game. Many people may not realize the true probability of statistics that will guarantee that they lose money over time.

Remember:

• Chances are always against the better

• The' home' always has the advantage, the' edge

'• The more you play, the more often you lose than you win.

Winning chances on' Pokies ' Pokies are expected to pay less than you put in them, so you'll lose the odds.

Through chance, poker machines are completely affected–that is, there is no way of knowing what the result will be. The more you're playing on a poker machine, the more likely you're going to lose.

The winner is always the poker machine. Myth: "I know that if I hit the button on the console at the right time, I can stop the reels at a powerful combination" Fact: Gaming machines are using software running a Random Number Generator (RNG). The RNG runs through numbers continuously. The RNG selects a combination at random at that specified microsecond when you press the play button. After this initial press, anything you do will have no impact on the outcome of the game.

Myth: "The individual who played the game after I won big I should have kept playing because that win was mine" Fact: any combination created by the gaming machine is completely random. This means that you cannot predict the next winning combination on a console. That spin is a random occurrence that has no impact on what has happened or is about to happen before.

Myth: "My gaming machine hasn't paid out for a while, so it's due to winning" Fact: a game's result is random and unpredictable. You can win the next spin, or you can lose the next one. It's completely random.

Myth: "When you bet in a certain pattern, you're more likely to win" Fact: each game's outcome is completely random.

Myth: "When I cash out after each win, my chance of winning will improve" Fact: A player who cashes out after each win has the same chance of winning as a player who does not cash out. Cashing out doesn't affect the outcome of the game.

Myth: "Some poker machines are luckier than others" Fact: -poker machine is just a computer programmed to produce random results.

Myth: "Gaming machines appear to pay out higher or more often at certain times of the day" Fact: All games outcome is random. Combinations that win or lose are not correlated with clocks or calendars.

Winning prospects on some forms of gambling in South Australia • Poker machines Winning 5 Black Rhinos on Black Rhinos Game (Top Prize) ($1 bet per line) Winning chances-1 in 9,765,625 • Lotto Winning First Division (playing 1 game) Winning chances-1 in 8,145,060 • Oz Lotto Winning First Division (playing 1 game) Winning chances-1 in 45,379,620 • Powerball Winning First Division (playing 1 game)

 Winning Odds Compared to Non-Gambling Related Activities

• Chances of experiencing depression in your lifetime ^- 1 in 7 people

• Chances of having mental illness each year-if you are a young Australian-1 in 4 people

• Marriage ending in divorce-1 in 2.3 marriages

- Chances of a man going bald-3 in 4 men

- Death from heart disease-1 in 4 people

- Stolen your car-1 in 4 people

- I've listed 20 of the most popular and fascinating gambling myths, but without too much effort, you can become able to come up with a list of another 20.

Although stopping gambling can sound like you're helpless, there are plenty of things you can do to solve the issue, restore your relationships and finances, and eventually regain control over your life.

Gambler's Psychology Gambling is an interesting social trend, and extensive research has been done on how gambling activity is influenced by psychological processes. Here are some interesting phenomena of gambling.

A recent study found a link between things that cause a positive mood (# of sunny days; local sports teams ' success) and increased gambling. The theory was that more risk-taking benefits from a positive mood.

Gambler's fallacy So, when 7 black numbers come up in a row, a roulette player watches, so he puts all his money on red. This well-known psychological process is called the fallacy of the gambler and is the mistaken belief that a particular occurrence is inevitable if an event occurs frequently. In fact, there are always the same chances of any particular event occurring.

Shifting expectations of winning, in a clever test, racetrack bettors were asked to measure the chances of winning their favorite horse pre and post betting on the horse. Gamblers appeared to assume that their horses had a greater chance of winning after making their bets than they had before betting. We were more optimistic because of the increased effort.

If lottery jackpots hit record levels and attract a lot of media attention, there's a frenzy of buying tickets when people decide they don't want to be left out of the loop.

Even people who have never played the lottery before at these times will "jump on the bandwagon" and purchase some tickets.

By its very nature, gambling structures and superstitions Gambling is a random event. However, many gamblers firmly believe they can build a winning gambling scheme. It involves trying to predict trends in random numbers (there are no), choosing "hot" slot machines and avoiding "cold" ones (e.g., continuing to play a machine because it's "hot;" playing a machine that has not paid off in a long time, believing it's "due"), or performing some ritualistic activity to keep winning (I know of several gamblers who hit slot machines with a lucrative one).

Gambling can be incredibly addictive, as you know, and often these psychological processes work to intensify the addiction. Studies in neuroscience showed that addiction to gambling has many of the same neural processes as an addiction to drugs.

The best way to break an addiction to gambling is by breaking down gambling mistakes and learning how to handle addiction. There are a lot of good websites and hotlines, including the National Council on Problem Gambling, to help deal with gambling addiction.

The National Council on Welfare (1996) analyzed the findings of eight Canadian adult prevalence studies in an attempt to identify a problem gambler's profile as described by other studies of the male gender. The study found a fairly consistent trend between male, single, and under the age of 30 years of problem gambling. Young adults (18-24 years of age) were nearly twice as likely to have moderate to serious gambling problems in the Ontario prevalence study as the general population (7% vs. 3.8%).

Similarly, Korn (2000) found in his study of prevalence studies that being white, young, and having concurrent substance abuse or mental illness put people at higher risk for gambling-related issues.

Financial restrictions In the NORC report (1999), problem gamblers were more likely to be on social assistance than non-problem gamblers, declared unemployment, had mental illness problems, sought mental health care in the previous year, and were convicted or incarcerated.

Race, age, and parental background Volberg and Abbott (1994) found that race, sex, parental history (a parent with a gambling problem), marital status, and household size were the variables that most discriminated between the coupled problem-pathological and non-problem classes.

Emotional Factors and Depression A number of studies directly explored the relationship between emotional states and levels of gambling (Jacobs, 1986; 1987; Rosental, 1993). Nonetheless, because this work appears to focus on cross-sectional designs, it is difficult to establish with any precision the temporal sequence of gambling and various emotional indicators. McCormick et al. (1984) explored the association between diagnosable influence and pathological gambling disorders. The sample consisted of 50 admitted pathological gamblers to an inpatient treatment program for gambling. Of the overall study, there was a major depressive disorder in 38 patients (76 percent). An interesting question, as noted by the authors, is whether depression creates inspiration to escape this feeling via gambling or whether the losses of gambling create depression. Participants in the study group were unable to reliably report the temporal relationship between early gambling and early episodes of depression.

Beaudoin and Cox (1999) looked at the characteristics of 57 adults looking for gambling issues treatment. Around
30% of the sample in the past reported receiving mental health services, most usually for depression. In addition, gambling was reported by 40 percent of the sample to rid unpleasant feelings. Such results suggest that gambling can serve as a tool for dealing with depression for some people. Pathological gambling is often associated with other behavioral problems, including the misuse of drugs, mood disorders, and personality disorders (Blaszczynsk & Steele, 1998; NORC, 1999).

Co-morbidity-Depression and depression

An important yet complicating element in the evaluation of the cause of this condition is the shared occurrence of two or more medical disorders, called co-morbidity. Is issue or pathological gambling a particular disorder that occurs alone, or is it merely a symptom of a social predisposition that underlies all addictions, hereditary or otherwise? Recently, the Manitoba Addictions Foundation's extensive longitudinal and open-ended interviews with problem gambling clients found that, in addition to depressive feelings, many problem gamblers reported playing in bars and casinos to relieve their intense sense of loneliness. A study of women with gambling problems by Brown 6and Conventry (1997) found that women's gambling motivations were boredom, depression, and isolation. Trevorrow and Moore (1998) found that women who had gambling problems were significantly loner (more distanced) than non-gamblers and non-problem gamblers. Researchers conclude that their study is "suggestive of loneliness (or alienation) as either a consequence or a weakness factor in problem gambling, but it would require a longitudinal research design to explain this question" (Trevorrow and Moore, 1998: 263).

Adverse Life Experiences Stressors in life were also described as an important component in gambling problem growth. The General Theory of Addictions (Jacobs, 1986) indicates that certain aspects of personality and life events affect the development of gambling issues. Jacobs argues that a history of adverse childhood experiences may lead to excessive gambling. In addition, some scholars have correlated psychological insecurity with negative experiences of inadequacy, inferiority, low self-esteem, and rejection in childhood (McCormick et al., 1987; McCormick et al., 1989). Research by Taber et al. (1987) found that 23 percent of the 44 admitted to an inpatient gambling treatment program had experienced severe trauma during their lifetime, and another 16 percent had reported moderately severe trauma. In addition, those with traumatic experiences have reported higher rates of drug abuse, depression, and anxiety relative to those without these experiences.

Social Factors Strong or weak networks of social support may improve recovery or an addiction to gambling. Addiction research has found some of the protective factors against addiction to be strong family or friendship ties and the general presence of family and friends in the life of the affected person (AADAC, 2001). The present research adds to the limited knowledge available by using a longitudinal design to track health and adjust the level of gambling problems over a span of one year. The research also offers detailed information on the general population's relationship between depression, anxiety, isolation, life events, and levels of social support and gambling.

Identical Psychological and Social Patterns A study revealed the effect of psychological, social, and environmental influences on gambling problems: Psychological Influences / Feelings Lack self-confidence Drug abuse Male gender Social Factors Family risk.

Environmental Factors

Media advertising Gambling venues are available. These factors have contributed to problem gambling among high school students in Addis Ababa, Ethiopia. Global gambling studies show similar risk factors for problem gambling, including male gender, risk looking for patterns, low self-esteem, depression and suicide ideation; social factors like peer pressures and parental gambling; and environmental factors such as gambling ads have been found to be positively correlated with problematic gambling spectrum.

Additionally, the study explored various types of adolescents engaged in gambling activities. Research findings revealed that playing cards, flipping coins, pool gambling, and PlayStation are the most frequently played gambling types among high school students, whereas Internet gambling is one of the least recorded.

In their analysis of adolescent gambling in the Australian Capital Territory (ACT) of students aged 7 to 12 years, Delfabbro et al. (2005) revealed that private card games (39.8%) and bingo/scratchies (40.5%) were the most commonly reported gambling activities whereas betting on racing and sporting events were also common (32% and 26% respectively). In some other study conducted between many teenagers in Oregon (Carlson and Moore, 1998), buying raffle tickets (41%) was the most frequently cited gambling practice, followed by betting on sports of friends or relatives (32%); playing cards (31%) and betting on skill games such as pool or bowling (25%).

Adolescent Gambling Addiction Factors: A BioPsychosocial Approach Adolescent gambling addiction has often been referred to as "secret addiction" because:

- No visible signs or symptoms such as other addictions (e.g., alcoholism, heroin addiction, etc.)

- Money scarcity and debts can be easily explained in a materialistic society

- Adolescent gamblers do not feel that they are addicted.

Addictions are always the product of experience and interplay between many variables, including the biological and/or genetic predisposition of the individual, their psychological state, their social environment, and the very nature of the behavior. Gambling is not a single trend, but a multifaceted phenomenon. Consequently, in many ways and at different levels of study (e.g., biological, social, or psychological), several factors can come into play. Central to the new theory is that no single degree of study is considered adequate to clarify either the gambling behavior's etiology or maintenance. In addition, this view states that all work is context-bound and should be examined from a viewpoint that is mixed or bio-psychosocial. Variations in gamblers ' attitudes and features and in gambling behaviors themselves indicate that results in one setting are unlikely to be important or true in another.

Structure of Gambling Activities The structure of gambling activities is another key factor in understanding gambling activity. Gambling behaviors have been shown to vary significantly in their structural characteristics such as the likelihood of winning, the amount of gambler participation, the use of close wins, the amount of skill that can be applied, the duration of the stake-outcome period, and the extent of possible wins. Structural variations are also found in certain groups of activities such as slot machines, where discrepancies in the frequency of reinforcement, colors, sound effects, and features of machines may significantly influence the machine's usability and attractiveness. Each of these structural features (and almost certainly does) has consequences for the motives of gamblers and gambling habits ' possible "addictively."

Duration The duration of the game is another essential structural aspect of gambling, namely, the length of the stake-outcome interval. Continuous behaviors (e.g., cycling, slot machines, and casino games) with a higher play rate have been found to be more likely to be correlated with gambling issues in almost all studies. In short time periods, the ability to make regular stakes increases the amount of money that might be lost and also increases the likelihood that gamblers will not be able to control spending. These issues are seldom found in non-continuous operations, such as weekly or biweekly lotteries, where gambling happens less regularly, and results are often uncertain for days. Therefore, it is significant to recognize that if the expanded operations are continuous rather than non- continuous, the overall social and economic effect of the growth of the gambling industry will be significantly greater. Other structural factors and dimensions reported in the overall gambling literature (external to the person itself) include:

- Stake size (including affordability issues, perceived value for money)

- Event frequency (i.e., the time gap between each game)

Amount of money earned in a given time period (important in chasing); reward systems (i.e., number and amount of prizes)

- Probability of winning 1 in 14 million on a 6/49 lottery

- Jackpot size over £ 1 million on a lottery

- Skill and pseudo-skill elements real or perceived

- "Near miss" opportunities (number of near winning positions)

- Light and light effects (e.g., u.

Each of these discrepancies can have consequences for the motives of an adolescent gambler and the social impact of gambling as a result. It /must be noted, but that many of these structural characteristics that cause gambling are dependent on single factors such as biological/genetic predispositions and personality factors.

Situational characteristics

The situational characteristics of gambling behaviors are other aspects that are central to understanding gambling activity. These are the factors that often make playing in the first place simpler and encouraging people. Situational features are mainly environmental features (e.g., accessibility factors such as location of the gambling venue, number of locations in a specified area and potential membership requirements) but may also include internal features of the venue itself (decoration, heating, lighting, color, background music, floor layout, refreshment facilities) or encouraging factors that may be relevant to the situation. In both the initial decision to play and the maintenance of the actions, these variables may be significant. Although many of these situational characteristics are assumed to affect susceptible gamblers, very little empirical work has been done on these factors and more research is needed before any conclusive conclusions can be drawn on the direct or indirect effect on gambling activity and whether vulnerable individuals are more likely to be influenced by these specific types of ma

One consequence of the recent rise in adolescent gambling research is that we can now begin to put together a "risk factor model" of those individuals who may be at the greatest risk of developing addictive gambling trends. A number of specific risk factors appear in the creation of problem adolescent gambling based on the previous description and empirical research literature summaries. Adolescent problem gamblers are more likely to:

• Be male (16–25 years of age)

- Have started gambling at an early age (as young as 8 years of age)
- Have had an earlier major win in their gambling careers

- Consistently chase losses

- Have started gambling with or alone with their parents

- Be anxious before gambling

- Be nervous and excited during gambling

- Be irrational (i.e., have misperceptions)

This list is not exhaustive but includes what is known empirically and anecdotally about gambling for adolescent issues. In addition, many of the risk factors involved in adolescent problem gambling have been believed to be very close to the risk factors involved in adolescent drug abuse (i.e., family history, low selfesteem, depression, history of abuse, etc.).

Although a change of personality has been recorded in young gamblers, many parents may attribute the change to adolescence itself (i.e., evasive behavior, mood swings, etc. are commonly associated with adolescence).

This is quite often the case that, once their son or daughter is in trouble with the police, many parents do not even know they have a problem. There are a number of possible signs of alarm to watch for, although many of these symptoms could be put down to puberty on an individual basis. However, if some of them apply to a child or adolescent, they might have a problem with gambling. The symptoms include:

A sudden decrease in the quality of schoolwork

- Going out every night and being evasive about where they were

- Mood changes such as being sullen, moody, or always on the defensive • Money missing from home

- Selling costly things and not being able to account for the money

- Loss of interest in hobbies they used to love

- Lack of concentration

Chapter 4: Problem and Compulsive Gambling: Signs, Symptoms, and Causes

Problem Gambling or Compulsive Gambling or Impulse Control Disorder

Gambling is harmless fun for many people, but it can turn into an issue. This form of compulsive behavior is often referred to as "problem gambling." A gambling problem is a progressive addiction that can have a lot of negative psychological, physical, and social effects. It is in the Diagnostic and Statistical Manual of the American Psychiatric Association (APA), fifth edition (DSM-5). Psychological and physical wellbeing is detrimental to problem gambling. People living with this addiction may experience depression, migraine, nausea, intestinal disorders, and other problems associated with anxiety.

The effects of gambling, as with other addictions, can lead to feelings of disappointment and hopelessness. In some cases, this may lead to suicide attempts.

Gambling addiction has become a major public health issue in many countries due to its harmful consequences.

Gambling addiction is a psychological-health problem that is known to be one of many types of problems of impulse-control and many similarities to obsessive personality disorder. Nonetheless, being more common to other addictive disorders is now known. The forms of gambling that could involve people with this condition are as complex as the available games. Betting on football, buying lottery tickets, playing poker, slot machines, or roulette are just a few of the compulsive gamblers ' habits. The place of choice for people with a gambling addiction also varies. While many prefer gambling in a casino, with the increasing use of the Internet, the online / Internet gambling addiction rate continues to rise. Conversely, certain compulsive players may also make risky investments in the stock market. Addiction to gambling is known as compulsive gambling or pathological gambling.

Problem Gambling as an addiction is a crippling condition that causes depression and anxiety.

The sensation of gambling is equivalent to taking a drug or having a drink for someone with a gambling addiction. Gambling behavior changes the mood and state of mind of the person. We keep repeating the behavior as the individual becomes accustomed to this feeling, trying to achieve the same effect.

For example, the individual begins to develop tolerance in other addictions, alcohol. The same "buzz" needs an increasing amount of alcohol. An adult who is addicted to gambling wants to play more to get the same high. They "chase" their losses in some cases, hoping they could win back lost money if they continue to engage in gambling. There are a vicious circle and an increased desire for activity. The strength to avoid decreases at the same time. The ability to control the urge to play is weakened as the craving increases in intensity and frequency.

This can have a professional, political, physical, social, or psychological impact. Neither the gambling frequency nor the amount lost will decide whether gambling is an individual problem. Many people engage rather than frequently in daily gambling binges, but the emotional and financial consequences will be the same. Gambling becomes an issue whenever the individual is no longer able to stop doing it and causes a negative effect on any area of the life of the individual.

Statistical Proof Estimates of the number of people who play socially and qualify for a gambling addiction diagnosis vary from 2% to 3%, impacting millions of people in the USA alone. Other important statistics on problem gambling include that it tends to have an international impact on at least 1 percent of people. In fact, teenagers tend to suffer from this condition twice as much as adults.

Although it is thought that more men than women suffer from pathological gambling, women are developing this disorder at higher rates, now accounting for as much as
25 percent of pathological gambling individuals. Other statistics about compulsive gambling are that during their early teenage years, men tend to develop this disorder, while women tend to develop it later. Then, though, women's disorder tends to get worse at a much faster rate than men. Many seemingly gender-based gambling addiction disparities include men's tendency to be addicted to more relational types of gaming, such as blackjack, craps, or poker, while women tend to participate in less interpersonal betting, such as slot machines or bingo. Men with pathological gambling tend to receive advice less often than their female counterparts on issues other than gambling.

Problem gambling generally involves gambling involving more than one symptom but less than the five or more symptoms required to qualify for compulsive or pathological gambling diagnosis. Binge gambling is a subtype of compulsive gambling that involves gambling problems, but only for certain periods of time. This is different from a general addiction to gambling, which appears to include excessive gambling activity regularly and to include recurrent thoughts (concern) about gambling, even when the individual is not involved in gambling.

Scientific and biological research on obsessivecompulsive factors and pathological gambling in an Italian study Gambling activity tends to be repetitive and difficult to avoid and seems to be directed at neutralizing or minimizing negative feelings such as anxiety and stress, indicating its similarities to the obsessivecompulsive continuum.

Based on gambling habits and obsessive-compulsive attitudes, a study of 300 Italian subjects was evaluated. The test took place in small centers in Italy, primarily in coffee and cigarette shops where slot machines are situated, using the South Oaks Gambling Screen (SOGS) and the MOCQ-R, a shortened version of Maudsley Obsessional-Compulsive Questionnaire.

A negative association between SOGS and MOPQ-R was observed in most of the subjects tested with respect to the control and cleaning subscales. Both instruments that evaluated demonstrated reliability and a strong capacity for discriminative purposes.

The study showed that the group of gamblers we studied did not belong to the field of obsessive-compulsive disorders, confirming the validity of the DSM-5 model for PG classification. Similar findings reflect the value of engaging in similar therapies to those used for conditions of drug use.

4.1 Pathological gambling

It is defined as a maladaptive and reoccurring pattern of gambling behaviors that persists despite significant negative effects on individuals, their work, and their families. This destructive conduct is often associated with increased psychological, legal, and financial issues. The prevalence of this social activity in Italy is rising as it has been estimated that at least once in a year, 54 percent of the Italian adult population (between the ages of 18 and 74) is gambling. There are nearly 30 million gamblers divided into different categories of sports, and in four years, the use of money for gaming, betting, and raffling has risen from € 6,000 million to € 17,000 million.

For teenagers, PG has also been identified, presenting important prevention issues. DSM-5 currently includes PG in the category of addictive disorders: it is referred to as a gambling disorder (GD) and is the only new addiction included, being the only one "without a drug." GD has many parallels with substance use disorders (SUDs), such as gradual loss of control over behavior, desire for euphoric or "strong" state, addiction, resistance, and symptoms of withdrawal. Often identified were the biological bases of PG, which is one of the reasons for its inclusion in the DSM-5 addiction portion.

PG also has many parallels to obsessive-compulsive disorder (OCD), but no less significant. Nevertheless, until the new manual was written, the discussion on how to classify PG, whether as an addictive disorder or as an obsessive-compulsive spectrum disorder, remained open.

Some scholars developed the idea of obsessivecompulsive related disorders in the early

1990s and applied to a class of conditions that share similarities with OCD. OCD is the compulsive disorder form. Obsessions are defined as recurring and persistent thoughts, perceived as intrusive by the subject. Compulsive behaviors are defined as goal-directed action that is repetitive, rigid, and stereotyped; individuals refer to being driven to perform them to avoid or reduce perceived negative effects. The gambling problem described in the DSM-5 resembles the obsessive thoughts usually found in patients suffering from OCD; in addition, the gambling activity tends to be repetitive and difficult to avoid and seems to be directed at neutralizing or minimizing negative moods such as anxiety and stress, again indicating parallels with OCD.

It was proposed that addiction compulsiveness arises from a dysregulation of particular neurochemical elements involved in brain reward and stress systems. The allostatic mechanism between reward function loss and brain stress system replacement provides a powerful basis for the creation of negative states that lead to compulsive behaviors (negative reward).

One theory suggests including the anhedonia factor of compulsive behavior. The loss of hedonic ability, possibly resulting in an underlying neuropsychological disorder, may be crucial in deciding the participation in regular and prolonged episodes of gambling, which, given negative consequences, reflect a compensatory effort to counterbalance tonic anhedonia. This theory was also suggested for other forms of addiction.

From different perspectives, the relationship between gambling disorder and obsessive-compulsive disorder was studied. Most research has to do with the phenomenological aspects of these two disorders.

Several pieces of researches also compared PG and OCD from the viewpoint of personality, finding differences in the dimensions of personality, and pointing out that patients with PG and OCD share similar profiles.

In 1999, Blaszczynski evaluated the presence of obsessions and compulsions in PG subjects using the Padua Inventory and highlighted specific outcomes of obsessiveness in pathological gamblers compared to subjects of control. On the other hand, the results were not confirmed by Won Kim and Grant's study, and other studies reported that PG shares more similarities with SUDs than OCD. Further research has also shown that other dimensions, such as the search for novelty and self-transcendence, are present. In addition, in an attempt to integrate knowledge in the field of pathological gambling, a 2008 review proposed a new theoretical model of three specific PG subtypes, which could be useful in finding more suitable treatments for the different subtypes. The obsessive-compulsive subtype is one of the three, different from the addictive subtype and the impulsive subtype. The authors pointed out that the OC subtype involves around 20-25% of players, mainly women, who establish gambling behaviors in reaction to negative psychological conditions, indicating that this group may respond better to antidepressants, SSRIs, and psychotherapy-related SNRIs.

A more new study, performed on an Italian sample, evaluated the prevalence of players of the different subtypes, showing a strong but not predominant presence of the OC subtype in the sample population; researchers also considered a possible combination of the different subtypes, indicating the effectiveness of different treatments for each of them. Differentiating into subtypes, as previously described in other research, is probably the right way to assess drug dependencies.

4.2 Gambling Addiction Signs and Symptoms

Gambling addiction is a form of the impulse-control disorder where you have little or no control over your gambling compulsion, even if you are conscious that your actions will harm you and others and even if the odds are against you.

There is often an underlying issue that causes you to continue playing games. Examples may include stress caused by work-related problems, unresolved relationship issues, drug or alcohol abuse, or a type of bereavement escapism, or any difficult emotional time in your life.

At first, we understand that it can be difficult at first to recognize that you have a gambling problem and to seek help. Whether you've lost a significant amount of money on one bet or over a period of time, your addiction to gambling can be corrected regardless of how severe your habit is.

Feeling a relentless urge to play even in a difficult financial state, or gambling as a way out of financial problems are both common symptoms of gambling addiction. Gambling addiction may also cause problems in relationships and at work, while the cost of financing a gambling addiction can become both an enormous burden and emotional pressure.

Excessive gambling emotional symptoms also trigger a variety of emotional symptoms, including anxiety, depression, and even suicidal thoughts and impulses. Such feelings can lead a gambler in extreme situations to actually make an attempt to end their lives. Losing all to gambling is devastating and leaves a lot of people feeling helpless.

Since gambling can cause depression, anxiety, and selfharming behavior, there are several physical signs of being identified. Depression and anxiety often contribute to lack of sleep, which under the eyes can lead to skin getting pale, weight gain or weight loss, acne, and dark circles.

4.3 Causes and Risk Factors for Gambling Addiction

It is vital to understand that there is generally no specific cause for pathological gambling when considering why people are playing. Several potential examples include the finding that in order to develop impulse-control disorders such as compulsive gambling, shopping, or compulsive sexual behaviors, several individuals given drugs to cure Parkinson's disease or restless leg syndrome were observed. The explanation of this relation includes the increased activity in the brain of the chemical messenger dopamine. One example that compulsive gambling may have a single cause is bipolar disorder because of exorbitant expenditure, including compulsive gambling, maybe a mania symptom that is part of bipolar disorder.

Much more generally, gambling addiction is described as the result of a combination of biological factors, ways of thinking, and social stressors (bio-psychosocial model), like most other emotional disorders. Nevertheless, there are elements that make the person more likely to develop a gambling addiction. Schizophrenia, mood problems, antisocial, alcohol and personality disorder, or drug use are risk factors for the development of pathological gambling. Individuals with low serotonin levels in the brain are also thought to be at higher risk compared to others for developing pathological gambling.

People who are suffering from compulsive gambling tend to be seekers of excitement, feel disconnected (dissociated), happy, or excited while playing video games or playing. Research also shows that individuals with money problems early in gambling earn a large amount of money, suffer a recent loss (such as divorce, job loss), or are lonely increases the risk of compulsive gambling. Easy access to gambling (e.g., living near towns with plenty of gambling resources, such as Las Vegas or Atlantic City), believing that they have discovered a winning gambling system and attempting to keep a record of money won and lost gambling are much more risk factors for compulsive gambling.

Causes as Cataloged by the DSM-5 the development of gambling disorder may begin in puberty or young adulthood, but it occurs in middle or even older adulthood in other individuals. Gambling behavior usually progresses over the years, although in females, the development tends to be quicker than in males. Many people who develop a gambling problem display a gambling trend that gradually increases both in frequency and wagering numbers Milder types will, of course, grow into more serious cases.

Many people with gambling disorder claim that one or two types of gambling are most troublesome for them, even though some people are involved in many forms of gambling. Individuals are likely to engage more often in certain forms of gambling (buying daily scratch tickets) than others (playing weekly casino slot machines or blackjack). Gambling frequency can be more related to the type of gambling than to the nature of the gambling condition as a whole. Buying a single scratch ticket every day, for example, may not be troublesome, while less regular casinos, sporting, or card gaming may be part of a gambling condition. Likewise, in terms of gambling behavior, amounts of money spent on wagering are not in themselves. Some people may wager thousands of dollars a month and have no gambling problem, while others may wager much smaller amounts but experience significant gambling-related difficulties.

Gambling trends may be frequent or episodic, and the disorder of gambling may be persistent or in relapse. During periods of stress or depression, and in periods of use or abstinence, gambling can increase. There may be extreme gambling periods and serious issues, times of complete abstinence, and un-problematic gambling periods. Spontaneous, long-term remissions are sometimes associated with gambling illness. However, some people underestimate their susceptibility to developing a gambling disorder or returning to a gambling disorder after remission.

Early gambling disorder presentation is more prevalent among males than for females. People who start playing games with youth often do so with family members or friends. Early-life gambling disorder progression seems to be associated with impulsiveness and misuse of drugs. Most high school and college students who develop gambling disorder over time mature out of condition, although for some, it remains a lifelong problem, the onset of gambling disorder in mid-and later-life is more common among women than among men.

The type of gambling behaviors and the incidence levels of gambling illness differ in age and gender. In younger and middle-aged people, gambling disorder is more common than in older adults. The disease is more common in males than females among adolescents and young adults. Younger people prefer different forms of gambling (sports betting), whereas older adults are more likely to develop slot machines and bingo gambling problems. While the proportion of individuals seeking gambling disorder care is small across all age groups, it is particularly unlikely that younger individuals will seek treatment.

Males are more likely to start gambling early in life and have a younger age than females who are more likely to start gambling later in life and acquire gambling disorder in a shorter period of time. Females with gambling disorders are likely to face depressive, bipolar, and anxiety disorders than males with gambling disorders. Females also have a later age at the onset of the disorder and seek treatment earlier, despite low rates of seeking treatment among people with gambling disorder regardless of gender.

Common signs of gambling addiction may be triggered by underlying stress associated with a stressful time in your life, whether a job, relationship or financially related, as well as having an addictive personality prone to compulsive behavior.

There are also underlying emotional reasons that can contribute to the development and vicious cycle of compulsive gambling, including

- Overcoming social isolation by visiting betting shops or casinos

- Feeling a rush of adrenaline and dopamine as a' good' release of chemical brain

- Numb, uncomfortable emotions and issues that cannot be solved easily

- Boredom and a desire to spend time

- Losing a companion as a result of gambling addiction is quite common due to the pressures and stresses that the issue of gambling imposes on a partnership

- Workplace issues that could include an increased workload, lack of work or a general lack of concentration that makes it hard to complete tasks sufficiently

- Dissimulating the amount of money and time spent on family betting the stigma that is often involved with gambling problems leads to a lack of confidence and often more problems at home

Denial that you have a gambling problem is a big concern as the first step to rehabilitation is to acknowledge that you have a problem.

- Problem with gambling and loss of interest in other aspects of life, such as avoiding family responsibilities and focusing solely on gambling outcomes Pathological gambling includes chronic and recurring gambling problems that include several of the symptoms listed that are not the result of another mental health problem, such as during a manic episode:

4.4 Triggers

Gambling can lead to a range of issues, but it can happen to anyone with an addiction. No one can tell who is going to develop a gambling addiction.

Gambling conduct becomes a problem when it cannot be regulated and interferes with jobs, relationships, and the workplace. The person may not know for some time that they have a problem.

Many people who create a gambling addiction are considered responsible and reliable individuals, but some factors may lead to behavioral change.

These may include:

• Retirement

• Stressful
situations Work-
related stress
• Emotional upheavals, such as depression or anxiety

• Isolation

• Existence of other addictions

Environmental factors,

Such as friends or opportunities available, Studies have suggested that people with a propensity to develop another habit. A role may be played by genetic and neurological factors.

Many people affected by gambling may also have an alcohol or drug problem, possibly due to an addiction predisposition.

Some alcohol use was associated with a higher risk of compulsive gambling.

Secondary addictions may also arise in an attempt to reduce the negative feelings generated by addiction to gambling. Most people who play never encounter any other addiction, however.

There are a few factors
These include:
- Depression, anxiety or personality disorders

- Certain addictions, such as drugs or alcohol

- The use of other medications, such as antipsychotic medicines and dopamine agonists, related to a higher risk of gambling addiction

- Sex, it is more likely to affect men than women. Need to play for excitement

2 with growing amounts of money. Restlessness or irritability while attempting to stop playing

3. Repeated attempts to stop, regulate, or raising gambling

4 have been ineffective. Always thinking about playing games and making plans to play 5. Gambling 6 when you feel depressed. Going back to gambling after losing money

7. Lying to hide the activities of gambling

8. Because of gambling 9, having a relationship, or work problems. Depending on others for cash to spend on gambling

An overview of signs and symptoms take a deeper look at some of the symptoms described above: You can't stop those who are playing for fun limit themselves and their bets. Compulsive gamblers are struggling with both their spending time and money. Betting takes overtheir lives, and they are continually wagering. They're trying to quit, but they can't.

You're playing with money that you can't afford to lose problem gamblers don't end with "fun money" being set aside for betting. They use the money spent on taxes, insurance, or education for their children. They not only squandered their last penny at times but also borrowed money.

The interviewed psychologist Stacy said one of his patients had borrowed such unsavory money from sources that he would put the safety of his family at risk.

Your bets go beyond casual gamblers playing for fun and spending a couple of dollars to have a good time. For reasons other than enjoyment, gambling addicts place bets, often attempting to escape depression or other problems. Whatever problems you face, it's not the solution to gambling.

You try to recover losses by playing more. Have you tried repeatedly to get back the money by betting more that you lost gambling? Problem gamblers will see more betting as a financial loss solution than it is— throwing money at the problem.

You are playing with ever more money like other addictions; small pathological gambling may begin. Yet problem gamblers are not going to be happy to keep the stakes small or set limits. To feel the rush, they need to bet more and more.

Pathological gamblers don't quit gambling when their bank account runs dry; you go to lengths to find money to play. Instead, to find more money, they go to extremes. While this may stop borrowing, some problem gamblers use fraud, falsification, or other crimes to fuel their habit.

Before more important matters, you put gambling problem gamblers to allow their habit to prioritize other parts of their lives. A gambling addict may skip watching the soccer game of her child or missing time to hit the casino at work. Careers are thrown on the back burner, and relationships fail at the cost of their habit.

Gambling has a negative effect on your emotions. Though gambling can be an exciting experience, addicts can experience emotions that signify a problem, including:

- Frustration or disappointment when you've tried to quit and struggle

- Remorse feelings

- A decline in motivation

- The desire to celebrate an unexpected gambling occurrence. If you think you're addicted, there are steps to help you quit. The key to saving your career, relationships, and bank account is to take early action.

Complications and Negative impacts of Gambling Addiction Although as many as one-third of people suffering from pathological gambling can recover from the disease without any treatment, the potential damage that compulsive gambling can cause in the life of the patient and those around it clearly indicates that the potential positive implications outweigh the potential complications. Each year in the United States, as much as $5 billion is spent on gambling, with people who are addicted to gambling accumulating tens of thousands of dollars in debt. Bad effects that compulsive gambling can have on the victim include financial problems ranging from high debt, bankruptcy, or deprivation, to legal problems arising from fraud to prostitution, lust, attempt, or suicide completion. Most compulsive gambling sufferers experience medical problems associated with stress, such as insomnia, stomach ulcers, and other gastrointestinal problems, headaches, and muscle aches. Gambling addiction can have a variety of adverse family effects. Statistics show that families with compulsive gambling individuals are more likely to experience domestic violence and abuse of children. Kids of problem gamblers are at significantly higher risk of depression, behavioral problems, and misuse of drugs. One of the drawbacks of compulsive gambling care is that as many as two-thirds of people starting treatment for this condition delay premature treatment, whether it includes medication, counseling, or both.

A manic episode does not describe gambling activity better.

Gambling addiction affects 1 to 3 % of all-age people, men more often than women. It usually starts in men and later in women in puberty. Although casino and sports betting are limited to just a few states, there has been a proliferation of other gaming venues, including riverboat and Indian casinos, state and national lotteries, and Internet access to offshore sports and parlor betting. The connection has dramatically increased. Older adults are often more vulnerable to gambling losses than other age groups due to their reliance on fixed incomes and reduced ability to recover.

Those with pathological behavior in gambling often have alcohol and other drugs, depression, and anxiety issues. Individuals with pathological behavior in gambling also take suicide into account.

Individuals with pathological gambling behavior, including bankruptcy, divorce, job loss, and prison time, appear to have personal, social, and legal issues. Gambling stress can also lead to heart attacks in at-risk individuals. The right treatment can help to avoid many of these issues.

4.5 Gambling Addiction Facts and Effects

• Compulsive gambling affects2%-3% of Americans can involve a variety of ways and places to bet, and symptoms may differ slightly between males and females, as well as between adults and adolescents.

• While men tend to develop gambling addiction at a higher rate and younger than women, women now make more than one-quarter of all compulsive gamblers, and women's symptoms appear to escalate more quickly once compulsive gambling develops.

• The problem of gambling involves more than one but less than five symptoms of compulsive gambling as opposed to pathological gambling.

- Although the direct causes of compulsive gambling are unusual, the development of this disorder has been associated with manic episodes associated with bipolar disorder and certain medications that treat Parkinson's disease and restless leg syndrome.

Schizophrenia, mood problems, antisocial personality disorder, alcohol, or cocaine addiction are risk factors for pathological gambling.

- Diagnosis of compulsive gambling includes recognizing at least five signs suggesting impaired gambling impulse control and excluding any potential causes of behavior.

- Like any mental health condition, a successful diagnosis of gambling addiction requires a complete physical and psychological assessment, including a mental-state evaluation and sufficient laboratory tests to rule out other possible causes of the symptoms being observed.

- Compulsive gambling care typically uses more than one method, including psychotherapy, medications, financial counseling, support groups, 12-step programs, and selfhelp.

- Therapy is positive for the prognosis of recovery from compulsive gambling.

- While pathological gambling can be overcome in many individuals on its own, the devastating consequences it typically has on the social, family, legal and mental health status of the person suggest that therapy must be managed by anyone who is encouraged to seek assistance for this condition.

•   Compulsive gambling treatment generally involves mitigating risk factors and educate the public on the warning signs of this condition.

Short-Term and Long-Term Effects of a Gambling Addiction

Gambling is associated with many more short-and longterm effects. Addiction to gambling also leads to other addictions that serve as coping mechanisms for people overwhelmed by the practice. Most gamblers turn to drugs, alcohol, and other behaviors to relieve the anxiety caused by the lifestyle of gambling. Even if a gambler never suffers financial ruin as a result of lifestyle, after self-medicating to deal with stress, they can struggle with drug and alcohol addiction for the rest of life. Often, as a result of gambling, relationships are often permanently damaged.

Check or Self-Assessment for Gambling Addiction When you think you're having a gambling problem, ask yourself if you'd be all right now if you'd stopped playing. If you're nervous or you're not supposed to stop yet, you're likely to suffer from a gambling addiction. If you're not sure, though, call our hotline to talk to someone who can help you determine if you have a problem and need assistance in recovery.

Chapter 5: Effects on Family and Relationships

5.1 Effects of Problem Gambling on Families

Intimate partners and other family members, including children, parents, siblings, and grandparents, are affected by gambling problems. Gambling issues affect family life and close relationships.

Impaired family relationships, emotional issues, and financial difficulties are some of the most common impacts of gambling problems on family members.

There is consistent evidence that gambling issues are associated with family violence.

The kids of problem gambling parents are at a much higher risk of developing gambling issues than the kids of non-problem parents.

The effects of gambling issues on intimate relationships were divided into three distinct phases:

(1) The denial phase,

(2) The stress phase, and

(3) The exhaustion phase (Custer & Milt, 1985).

Recent research indicates that people with gambling problems have intimate relationships involving poor communication, relationship and sexual dissatisfaction, conflict and disagreements, and the possibility of separation or divorce (Dowling, Smith, & Thomas, 2009; Hodgins, Shead, & Makarchuk, 2007).

Increased gambling Questions unpaid bills Depression

Phase Spouse spends less time with the family Arguments Spouse feels rejected Attempts to control gambling Exhaustion Phase Learning impaired Confusion Physical symptoms Immobilization Anger Anxiety and fear impact on children when they feel rejected Many kids may be neglected, discouraged, and frustrated. They might assume that they caused the problem and that the problem would stop if they are "healthy." Many kids are looking after younger brothers or sisters or trying to support their parents. Kids are overwhelmed by this obligation.

Kids may also feel that their parents have to take sides. We may cease to trust a parent who promises not to keep him or her. At school, they can steal from the parent or get into trouble. Many young people may attempt to draw attention away from the parent with the issue of gambling by• Using alcohol or other drugs • Gambling• Breaking the law. It is important to help children understand that their fault is not the problem of the family. It is important for children to return to a healthy and happy home life and a normal childhood. Family or individual counseling may help kids navigate these shifts.

Problem gambling and recent suicide research have shown a strong connection between gambling issues and suicidal thoughts—more than twice the number of people affected by gambling issues claim they consider taking their own lives compared to those not affected by gambling.

There is a limit to how much a person's body can take before they need medical intervention with other addictions, such as drugs or alcohol. Gambling isn't like that, and often for a long time, a downward spiral can go unchecked. Especially if there are large amounts of debt involved, there may seem to be no other option.

If you are self-harmed or have suicidal thoughts or feelings, it is important to seek professional assistance as soon as possible.

5.2 Impacts on Family Environments

Beyond intimate partners.

The family atmosphere of people with gambling problems is also marked by high levels of anger and confrontation as well as low levels of clear and effective contact, less freedom, less engagement in intellectual and cultural activities, lack of commitment and encouragement, little direct expression of feelings and less participation in social activities (Ciarrocchi & Such social dynamics are equivalent to drinking-problem people (Ciarrocchi & Hohmann, 1989). In addition, gambling-related children are exposed to a variety of family stressors, including financial and emotional deprivation, physical isolation, inconsistent supervision, parental neglect/abuse and rejection, inadequate role- modeling, family conflict, and diminished security and stability (Darbyshire, Oster, & Carrig, 2001).

Common Family Members Problems Common gambling issues reported by family members include:
• Loss of household or personal money

• Arguments

• Anger and violence

• Lies and deception

• Family neglect

• Neglected relationships

• Poor communication

• Confusion of family roles and responsibilities

• Development of family gambling problems or other addictions

• Many people.

• Friendships may end due to unpaid debts Relationship between Gambling Problems and Domestic violence There is now consistent global evidence that gambling issues are more closely linked to intimate partner violence (IPV) and domestic violence (Dowling et al., in press). Relationships are complex; however, people with gambling issues are more likely to be victims and perpetrators of IPV than people without gambling issues.

The World Health Organization (2002) describes IPV as any activity that causes physical, psychological, or sexual damage to those in that relationship within an intimate relationship. This may include physical abuse, sexual abuse, mental (psychological) abuse, and behavior management. As per a systematic review of globally available research (Dowling et al., in the press), more than one-third of individuals with gambling troubles report being victims of physical IPV (38%) or IPV (37%) perpetrators. In fact, 11% of IPV victims report gambling issues.

While most evidence relates to intimate relationships, there is some evidence that victimization and violence perpetration leads to children and other members of the wider family (Dowling, Jackson, et al., 2014; Dowling et al., in the press; Suomi et al., 2013). Over half of people to gambling problems (56%) report physical violence against their kids (Dowling et al., in press), according to the systematic review. In addition, several recent Australian studies have found that between one-third and one-half (34-53%) of people with gambling problems and family members experience any form of family abuse in the previous 12 months (victimization (27-41%), perpetration (23-33%); Dowling, Jackson, et al., 2014; Suomi et al., 2013). In these studies, the most common perpetrators and victims of family violence were parents, current partners, and former partners. Nevertheless, it is important to view with care the results of studies involving family members other than spouses. Only a few studies of recorded prevalence estimates are available with significant variability. Furthermore, many studies are not representative of the general population, include only a small number of problem gamblers, use categories that may encounter multiple problems in addition to issues related to gambling, and use different definitions of abuse. More research is needed to remind the family of the association between problem gambling and crime.

5.3 Effects on the Health and Wellbeing of Family Members

Intimate partners and children are adversely affected by gambling problems in various ways (Dickson-Swift, James & Kippen, 2005; Hodgins, Shead, et al., 2007; Vitaro, Wanner, Brendgen & Tremblay, 2008). There are common mental issues, physical ailments, and behavioral problems.

Emotional Disturbances of Intimate Partners Rage Resentment Depression Anxiety Emotional Disturbances of Children Depression Anxiety Confusion Guilt Physical Problems of Intimate Partners Symptoms

Gastrointestinal Disturbances Hypertension Physical Issues of Children Asthma Allergies Chronic symptoms Psychological Disturbances of Intimate Partners By taking on more tasks, one member can try to keep things under check. This may result in burnout. Family members frequently concentrate on the gambling problem individual and forget about taking care of themselves or having fun.

Passing Problem Gambling from one generation to the next the children of trouble gambling parents are also at risk of developing their own gambling problems. Findings from four independent studies investigating the intergenerational and family transmission of gambling issues found that people with a gambling problem having a parent or sibling is two to ten times more likely to experience gambling issues than people without a parent or sibling with a gambling problem. Individuals with gambling problem fathers were 11 to 14 times more likely to have gambling problems, and people with gambling problem mothers were 7 to 11 times more likely to have gambling problems.

Risk factors

- Gambling at a young age

- Parental drug and mental health problems

- Personal drug use

- Gambling to reduce negative emotions or increase positive emotions • Gambling for socialize

- Expecting gambling will lead to positive outcomes (e.g., feelings of control or financial gain) Protective factors

- Being female

- Having increased social resources and networks

- To have more siblings

- Expecting gambling will lead to negative outcomes (e.g., depression or over-involvement

Financial Impact on the Gambler

There is a reason why people consider problem gambling addiction–it can be really hard to stop, close to a chemical addiction to nicotine or another drug in some ways. This is because when gamblers win, dopamine, a chemical in our brain that makes us feel happy, appears to be released. This chemical reaction in the brain is one of the factors contributing to addiction feelings, and other brain-related factors may also be involved. Dr. Franco Manes, a neurological researcher, suggests that impairments in the pre-frontal cortex of the brain may make it harder for a problem gambler to consider future consequences accurately. Impulse management and decision-making by executives can also be impaired. Both biological and neurological factors can strongly tax an individual's gambling problem, causing severe stress, anxiety, or feelings of helplessness. Financial repercussions can also pile up, as Problem Gambling records these individuals losing around $21,000 a year– that's one-third of a nationwide average income. Because of the addictive chemical causes of gambling, it can be very difficult for a problem gambler to leave. Financial Effect on Family Members another AGRC study found that financial pressures, disrupted relationships, lack of trust, and other emotionally upsetting effects were the three most common negative effects of extreme gambling on families. The most common issue is money loss. You can suddenly lose your money, properties, or belongings. Such a money crisis makes the family feel afraid, furious and betrayed. A build-up of these negative emotions may cause relationships to break down. In reality, Problem Gambling focused on problem gamblers in a study on depression and relationship issues, finding that they are six times more likely to divorce, four times more likely to have problems with alcohol, and four times more likely to smoke regularly. One research by The Problem Gambling Treatment and Research Center showed that problem gambler children are ten times more likely to follow their parents ' footsteps once they become adults. The AGRC stresses that these conditions can leave family members and loved ones with adverse effects on their own health, particularly if their attempts to dissuade or change the gambling behavior of the problem fail. Such cases may benefit more from professional assistance so that all sides are considered equally, and the opinions of all are respected and treated carefully

Chapter 6: How can Family Rescue Problem Gambler and Control Finances

How to Help Loved One from Gambling If you have a gambling problem with your loved one, you probably have a lot of feelings that clash. You may have spent a lot of time and money trying to avoid cheating or having to cover your loved one for them. At the same time, you may be angry about your loved one again for playing games and sick of trying to keep up the charade. Your loved one may have borrowed or stolen money without any way of repaying it. They may have sold family property or worked on joint credit cards with huge debts.

Although compulsive and depressed gamblers need their family and friends ' support to help, they avoid gambling in their struggle, their decision to quit must be theirs. You can't make someone quit gambling as much as you want, and as hard as it sees the results. You should, however, empower them to seek help, assist them in their efforts, protect themselves, and take seriously any talk of suicide.

Preventing suicide in problem gamblers if a problem gambler faces the consequences of his actions, he can suffer a crippling decrease in self-esteem. This is one reason why compulsive gamblers have a high suicide rate.

Problem gamblers are much more likely to attempt suicide, according to a landmark report that sparked government calls to do more to counter the risks of gambling.

Studies conducted by Gamble Aware, a major UK gaming organization, found that problem gamblers were six times more likely to have suicidal thoughts or threaten to take their own lives–and might be 15 times more likely to do so.

Even when accounting for other contributing factors that could be related to suicidal thoughts such as depression, substance abuse, and financial problems, the elevated risk persisted.

The researchers found that excluding these causes, problem gamblers were still three times more likely to consider or attempt suicide.

Nearly one out of five, or 19 percent, had considered suicide in the past year compared to 4.1 percent of the general population, while 4.7 percent had attempted suicide compared to 0.6 percent in the broader population.

Dr. Heather, assistant professor at the London School of Hygiene and Tropical Medicine, co-author of the report, said the results of the study would cause swifter action to protect addicts, particularly within the industry.

"Gambling harms are significant and can be detrimental to persons, families, and communities; she said. These results show how people having gambling problems are a higher risk group for suicidality. "The people at the forefront of coping with this high-risk group are the industry, who need to think about how they prepare workers with encounters with suicidal people potentially. Charles and Liz Ritchie, who created the charity Gambling with Lives after their son Jack killed himself when he was addicted to gambling at the age of 24, said the study showed the need for greater government action.

The Ritchies want to hold the government legally liable for the death of their son, blaming the industry for lax regulation.

Identifying and addressing suicidal thoughts A family member may have thoughts of suicide if he or she:

- Changes in behavior, appearance or mood

- Seems depressed, sad or withdrawn

- Gives away precious possessions

- Talks about suicide and says that he or she has a plan

- Makes a will or talks about final wishes. If this happens, you should:
- Take all suicide threats seriously

- Stay calm and listen to care. Do not pass judgment or try to solve the issue

- Ask if the person feels suicidal and has a plan

- Remove all means of self-harm (e.g., weapons, medicines)

- Support the person in seeking professional assistance (e.g., crisis line, psychiatrist, doctor, emergency room or clergy)

- Keep your doctor be aware of what is going on

- Do not agree to keep the person's suicidal thoughts a secret

- Talk to someone who is willing to do so.

6.1 Tips for Family Members

Start by helping yourself

You have the right to emotionally and financially secure yourself. Do not blame yourself for the problems of the gambler or let your life be governed by his or her addiction. Ignoring your own needs may be a burnout formula.

Don't do it alone. It may be so difficult to deal with the gambling addiction of a loved one that it may seem easier to rationalize their desires "this last time." Or you may feel ashamed, feeling as if you are the only one that has issues like this. Reaching for help will make you realize that this dilemma has been faced by many families.

Set money management guidelines Consider taking over the family finances to ensure that the gambler remains responsible and to prevent a recurrence. This will not mean, however, that you are responsible for micromanaging the impulses of the problem gambler to play. Your first duty is to ensure that there is no danger to your own finances and credit.

Remember how demands for money are treated by problem gamblers often become very good to ask for money, either directly or indirectly. To obtain it, they may use begging, bribery, or even threats. It takes practice to ensure that you do not encourage the gambling addiction of your loved one.

Do's and Don'ts for Problem Gamblers Partners Do Talk to your partner if you're cool and not worried or upset about their problem gambling and its effects.

Look for support for families of problem gamblers such as self-help groups and reach out to people who have faced the same obstacles.

Explain to your partner that you are looking for help because you and your family are affected by their gambling.

Talk to your kids about the gambling issue of your parents.

Manage the family finances, track bank, and credit card statements carefully.

Encourage and support your loved one during the care of their problem of gambling, even if it may be a long process of setbacks.

Don't lose your temper, preach, teach, or make threats and ultimatums that you can't keep going.

Overlook the positive quality of your partner.

Prevent family life and events from affecting your partner.

Expect the recovery of your partner from the gambling problem to be smooth or quick. Even if their gambling ceases, there may be other underlying issues.

The bailout of debt or allow your partner to play in any way.

Hide or deny the problem of your partner to yourself or others.

Rationally Approaching the Loved One about gambling does not presume that gambling problems are a process through which the individual is likely to pass. When you believe that your spouse has gambling problems, it's important to help him because the implications can be major. These may involve a breakup of marriages, financial issues, criminal penalties, job loss, family violence, and mental health issues.

If you are worried and are upset by the gambling of your partner, you should:

- Choose a convenient time and place to talk.

- Make sure you have enough time and meet in a private space away from distractions and interruptions.

- It is also important to plan for gambling problems by providing information on support.

- You should talk to the loved one about his gambling issues in a calm and rational way.

- First, tell him and your friendship with him
  about some positive things.

- It's important to discuss what habits you've
  encountered, instead of concentrating on
  the individual as the issue.

- Remove comments that might suggest that
  you're judging.

- Use' I' statements instead of' you' statements, e.g.'
  I'm concerned when I don't know when you're
  coming home or how much money you're going to
  spend' rather than' You're frustrated when you're
  late and wasting all of our money.'

- Make recommendations instead of telling the
  person what to do, e.g.,' would you be comfortable
  seeing a gambling counselor?

- Ask the loved one for his viewpoint, thus validating
  his experience and emotions, e.g., "I understand that
  gambling is important to you."

- Give the person enough time to tell his story, as it
  will allow him to open up and trust you.

You should not:

Speak, question, or argue with the person about their
gambling issues

- Try to control the individual by threatening,
  bribing, crying, or nagging

- Use shame in an effort to force the person can change

- Attack the person verbally or physically. If you think that any negative attitudes towards the person's gambling or gambling, in general, hinder your ability to help the person, you should suggest that the person talks to someone else.

Be ready for the full range of responses you might receive, from relaxation to frustration, while talking to the loved one. The loved one may deny, minimize, rationalize, or lie about his problems with gambling, or blame others. Be aware that he or she may feel embarrassed or ashamed and may not want to speak. You are using empathy and compassion to reduce the chances of this happening. If the person doesn't want to talk about gambling issues, you can tell him or her about available gambling help, and you're willing to talk when he or she's ready. If the conversation becomes unproductive or aggressive, the discussion should be stopped, and you should try again.

Encouraging medical assistance Effective professional assistance for gambling issues is available. Not everyone needs or wants professional assistance, though. Treatment targets may be to abstain from gambling or to set limits on gambling practices. Familiarize yourself with the effective treatments available for gambling issues and encourage the loved one to seek the most appropriate type of help. You must also familiarize yourself with the available local resources to help people with gambling issues, so you can tell him or her about these when you talk to the loved one. These services may include professional gambling services, resources for self-help, support groups, mechanisms for self-exclusion, and culturally diverse services.

Since financial issues can be a major part of gambling, you should be aware of tools that can help your loved one solve financial problems. The loved one might also need to access other types of gambling-related issues such as medical assistance, legal services, mental health care, financial advice, vocational rehab, or social assistance. In pointing out that:

- Gambling problems can be successfully treated, you can motivate him or her to seek professional help for gambling issues. Professional help, support groups, and self-help approaches have helped many individuals with gambling problems.

- It is a sensible thing to seek help for a problem, rather than a sign of weakness.

- The earlier the question is dealt with, the faster it can be resolved.

- All medical aid shall be confidential.

Encouraging the family member to improve It is not your personal responsibility to' fix' the gambling problems of the individual. You should persuade the member of the family to improve, though. Do not expect the gambling habit to be moral about him or her or to change it immediately. Consult with the member of the family to decide on appropriate habits, such as talking to a therapist, staying within negotiated spending limits. Be clear about what you're able to do to support the family member and what habits you're going to tolerate, although you can change these limits over time.

- Think about the techniques that gambling companies use to keep people gambling and maximize profits, for example. Gaming machines are designed in a way to keep people playing and spending money

- Avoid going to gambling sites, even if they don't plan on gambling, for example, going to a pub for food where gambling is possible. These might include:

- Searching for encouragement from other family members, friends or others to help him reduce his gambling

- Eviting spending time with people associated with gambling habits

- Identifying and using ways to handle gambling impulses

- Setting and adhering to a budget

- If the family member is gambling online, using software programs that block or limit access

- Recognition

If this or any other self-help approaches are determined by the family member, offer to support him. Notice and congratulate him on any positive changes the person has made. It is important to focus on the future rather than past mistakes as the individual attempts to change his gambling. The person who stopped or reduced his gambling may notice a void in his life that was filled with gambling, e.g., reduction in social activities.

If that's the case, you can recommend things you can do with the person who doesn't include gambling (e.g., going to the movies or a restaurant) and reconnects with family and friends. Such social support can also relieve causes that can aggravate gambling issues like anxiety, frustration, stress, depression, or boredom.

6.2 Looking After your Finances

Money could be a sensitive subject for many people, and when there is a gambling problem, it can become even more sensitive. If you have a gambling problem with someone near you, you may need to secure your finances. These tips will help people and their circumstances for partners, family, and friends. Sometimes, when determining how to handle money issues, it's a good idea to talk to a financial advisor.

Protecting your Finances Family members are facing financial pressures from people with gambling problems. You may need to take on the role of looking after the finances of your family and managing access to money for your partner.

Together with a financial advisor, you might consider:

Having a family budget—try to make it realistic, especially when it comes to repaying debts so that the individual with a gambling problem does not feel the need for more gambling

- Careful monitoring of all family spending

- Managing family finances until the gambling is under control

- Agree on how much cash or loan your spouse has to pay.

- Thinking carefully about your own assets before offering financial assistance

- Paying bills yourself rather than lending money to bills

- Not sharing your PIN numbers

- Keeping your valuables and cash out of sight

- Warning your relatives, friends, and colleagues not to lend money to the individual

- Changing your will to ensure your potential wealth is not lost to gambling.

Strategies for Financial Management and Damage Control Lock your credit while "locking" a mutual credit account can temporarily prevent you from accessing your own funds, it will help prevent the situation from getting worse than it already has.

Open in your name only a new credit card and bank account

There are plenty of married couples who manage their finances completely separately. By removing your name from compromised accounts and creating new accounts that will only be open to you, you will prevent your loved ones from draining your funds while also ensuring that your credit score is safe.

Secure or move any of your long-term investments Gambling addicts are more likely to focus on long-term assets–college savings, retirement funds, holiday savings–as they will not have to deal with the consequences of these acts until much further down the road.

6.3 Speak with a financial advisor

In past situations similar to yours, professional financial advisors have undoubtedly worked with people. We may have expert advice about other actions that you can take.

If you're someone who has a gambling problem financially linked to the family member, it is significant to make sure that they do not have access to the resources that will make their problem worse. Many of these actions may, in the future, if necessary, be functionally "undone." Meanwhile, prevention of damage must be a top priority.

The above measures will help to prevent the situation from worsening. However, if the issue of gambling has existed for years, then other claims are likely to have to be addressed retroactively.

Here are a few things you can do to help get your financial situation back in order: arranging all your debts and consolidating debt restructuring, if possible, will help make your debts more manageable.

If you can pay this back in time, you can eventually be able to lower your monthly interest rates.

You are refinancing debts that are not especiallyurgent.

The prospect of refinancing is certainly worth considering whenever you are faced with an unforeseen source of financial obligations.

Help restore your reputation with a zero-interest credit card. If you have a gambling problem, your credit may need to be fixed.

Even if you only use the card for something as basic as a gum pack every month, it will help to improve your creditworthiness by regularly meeting such financial obligations.

Check for other financial sources Personal loans, government assistance, and additional income sources (entering the workplace or taking up a second job) are just a few of the ways you can boost the monthly cash flow of your family. In fact, it can aid you in different situations of refinancing.

Many lenders and credit card companies want you to be a client. Even if the current financial situation is less than optimal, as long as you are able to handle your loans responsibly, certain choices are likely to be within your control.

Chapter 7: Beating Gambling Addiction through Self-management

Self-Help for Problem Gamblers

The most significant step to overcoming an addiction to gambling is to realize you have a problem. To own up to this requires tremendous strength and courage, particularly if you've lost a lot of money along the way and strained or broken relationships.

Do not despair, and do not try to go it alone. Many others were in your shoes, breaking the habit and restoring their lives. You can do that, too.

Learn how to alleviate unpleasant feelings in healthier ways Are you playing when you're lonely or bored, after a stressful day at work, or after an argument with your spouse?

Gambling can be a means of calming, unwinding, or socializing unpleasant emotions.

There are safer and more effective ways to manage your moods and alleviate boredom, such as running, spending time with non-playing friends, taking on new activities, or practicing relaxation techniques.

Strengthen your support network without help it's hard to fight an addiction, so reach out to friends and family. There are ways to make new friends without depending on visiting casinos or online gambling if your support network is small. Try to reach out to co-workers, join a sports team or book club, participate in an education class or volunteer for a good cause.

For example, entering a peer support group Gamblers Anonymous is a 12-step recovery program based on anonymous alcoholics. A vital part of the program is to find a sponsor, a convicted gambler who has the experience that remains free of gambling and can provide you with invaluable guidance and support.

Depression, stress, substance abuse, or anxiety can both cause gambling problems and get worse by compulsive gambling. Even if gambling is no longer part of your life, these issues will remain, so resolving them is necessary.

For many problem gamblers, it's not stopping gambling but the biggest challenge is remaining in recovery making a lifelong commitment to stay away from gambling. The Internet has made gambling much more available and hence more difficult to rehab users in order to avoid recurrence. Digital casinos and bookmakers are available to anyone with a smartphone or computer access all day, every day.

If you surround yourself with people to whom you are accountable, avoid enticing environments and websites, give up control of your finances (at least at first), and pursue alternative activities to replace gambling in your life, sustaining recovery from gambling addiction or problem gambling is still possible.

Make Healthier Choices. One way to stop gambling is to remove and replace the conditions required for gambling to take place in your life with healthier choices.

The four conditions needed to continue gambling are a decision.

You need to make the decision to play for gambling to happen.

If you have an urge: stop what you're doing and call someone, think about the consequences of your acts, tell yourself to stop thinking about gambling, and find something else to do right away.

Without capital, money gambling can't happen. Get rid of your credit cards, let someone else be responsible for your money, get the bank to make automatic payments for you, close online betting accounts, and keep a limited amount of cash on you.

Time: you can't play online if you don't have the time. You have to prepare for your leisure time.

Find other ways to fill the quiet moments during your day if you're gambling on your mobile.

Gambling is a game in which there is no chance to play without a game or operation to bet.

Do not put yourself in situations that are enticing, tell gambling establishments that you often have a problem with gambling and ask them to restrict your admission. Disable gambling applications on your mobile and computer and block gambling sites.

Maintaining recovery from gambling addiction depends a lot on finding alternative behaviors to replace gambling. Some examples include:

To engage in a fun activity, get a rush of an adrenaline sport or a competitive task, such as mountain biking, rock climbing, or go-kart racing To be more social, overcome shyness or loneliness with counseling, join a public speaking class, enter a social group, interact with family and friends, volunteer, find new friends to numb unpleasant feelings, do not worry about problems.

Deep breathing, meditation, and massage solve many anxiety problems.

Prevent depression by contacting a trusted family member, meeting a friend for coffee, or going to a Gamblers Anonymous meeting the urge to play may pass or become weak enough to resist as you wait.

Visualize what happens if you succumb to the temptation to play. Talk about how you'll feel after all your money's gone and you've disappointed yourself and your family again.

Distract yourself with another task, such as going to the gym, watching a movie, or doing a gambling cravings relief exercise.

When you can't resist the temptation for gambling, don't be too harsh on yourself or use it as an excuse to give up.

It's a tough process to conquer a gambling addiction. From time to time, you will slip; the important thing is to learn from your mistakes and continue to work towards recovery.

Gambling Addiction Treatment these strategies may include compulsive gambling treatment:

7.1 Therapy

It may be useful for behavioral therapy or cognitive behavioral therapy. Behavioral therapy requires regular exposure to your unlearned actions and teaches you strategies to reduce the gambling urge.

Cognitive-behavioral therapy focuses on recognizing and changing good, optimistic, dysfunctional, unreasonable, and negative attitudes. It may also be helpful for family therapy.

Medicines Antidepressants and mood stabilizers can help with problems that often go hand in hand with compulsive gambling — like depression, OCD, or ADHD.

In reducing gambling activity, some antidepressants may be effective. Medicines called narcotic antagonists can help combat compulsive gambling, which is useful in treating substance abuse.

7.2 Self-help groups

Many people find that talking to others with a problem with gambling can be a valuable part of treatment. Ask for advice on self-help groups such as Gamblers Anonymous and other support from your health care professional.

Compulsive gambling services may include an outpatient program, hospital program, or residential treatment plan, depending on your needs and resources. Your compulsive gambling treatment plan may include medication for substance abuse, depression, anxiety, or any other mental health condition.

Relapse prevention you can return to gambling even with treatment, particularly if you spend time in gambling environments with people who play or you are in gambling.

 Tell your mental health professional or mentor right away to head off a relapse if you fear you're going to start gambling again.

It's never easy to overcome a gambling issue, and looking for professional treatment doesn't mean you're deficient in some way or can't handle your issues. Every gambler is special, so you need a recovery program specifically tailored to your needs and circumstance.

Tell your doctor or mental health professional about different treatment options, including hospital or residential treatment, and rehabilitation programs are aimed at people with a serious gambling addiction who cannot stop gambling without round-the-clock assistance.

Treatment for underlying conditions that lead to your compulsive gambling, like misuse of drugs or mental health issues including depression, anxiety, OCD, or ADHD This may include changes in therapy, medicine, and lifestyle. Problem gambling will sometimes be a symptom of bipolar disorder, so before making a diagnosis, the doctor or therapist may have to rule out this.

CBT cognitive-behavioral therapy for gambling addiction focuses on modifying the habits and perceptions of pathological gambling, like rationalizations and false beliefs. It may also teach you how to fight the impulses of gambling and solve health, job, and relationship issues caused by gambling problems. Therapy will give you the tools to cope with your life-long addiction.

Family therapy and marriage, career counseling, and credit counseling will help you work through the specific issues generated by your gambling problem and lay the foundation for fixing your relationships and finances.

Problem and Pathological Gamblers Interventions:

Pharmacotherapies Small to moderate, randomized, short-term, placebo-controlled, and, with the exception of one research, flexible-dose clinical trials have been performed over the past several years to examine the efficacy and tolerability of different pharmacotherapies in the treatment of pathological gambling.

Two selective serotonin reuptake inhibitors (SSRIs; fluvoxamine and paroxetine), a μ-opioid blocker (naltrexone), and a mood stabilizer (lithium) have been shown to be superior to placebo in the treatment of patients with pathological gambling in the short term.

Of these, SSRIs and naltrexone research excluded people with significant co-occurring mental health/substance use disorders (excluding nicotine dependence), and progress in gambling symptomatology and overall clinical status was found in the absence of significant changes in mood and anxiety measurements.

A lithium study only included bipolar spectrum participants with pathological gambling, excluding psychotic disorders, and progress in gambling, mania, and general clinical status indicators were observed. A placebo-controlled trial of the atypical antipsychotic drug olanzapine in the treatment of video poker pathological gamblers found no increased effectiveness over placebo, although variations in gambling severity intergroup measures at the beginning of the trial were complicated interpretations.

7.3 Successful Problem Treatment

Gambling with medications that decrease impulses and increase inhibitions. Researchers found positive results at the annual meeting of the American College of Neuropsychopharmacology (ACNP) in gamblers treated with drugs often used for opioid addictions. Individuals with chronic gambling disorder will continue their gambling activity in the face of their own and their families ' harmful consequences.

Dr. Jon Grant and his University of Minnesota team used cognition-measuring exercises to assess what motivates this intense gambling activity. They included men and women in one of three trials of medicine with a primary diagnosis of pathological gambling. Study sites ranged from 70 participants to 100 participants in number.

Scientists tried to understand how gamblers decide to bet on two brain processes: desire and inhibition.

In order to divide people into groups that reflect discrepancies in their physiology, Grant divided pathological gamblers into two main subtypes: gamblers motivated by compulsion (i.e., individuals who report gambling when temptation becomes too intense to control) and those who do not exhibit normal regulation of impulsive activities (i.e., individuals who report being unable to regulate behavior).

In the first subtype, urge-driven gamblers reacted well to treatment with drugs that block the opioid brain system (e.g., naltrexone) or some neurotransmitter glutamate receptors (e.g., meantime). Grant also found that family history plays a significant role in further refining this group.

 Those with a family history of addiction reacted much better to the opioid blocker, which was shown to lessen the temptation to use drugs like alcohol in other studies.

The second subtype, gamblers who have trouble inhibiting their actions and responding to the slightest impulses, respond well to drugs that operate on a particular enzyme, catechol-O-methyl-transferase (COMT), which plays a major role in the prefrontal cortex work. Researchers found that decreasing COMT's function could increase one's ability to inhibit one's willingness to play.

"We can approach the central biology of the disorder with individualized care by recognizing these various subtypes," said Jon Grant, MD, JD, MPH, Associate

Professor of Psychiatry at the University of Minnesota and a member of ACNP. "If we look at pathological gambling as an addiction and try to understand the nature of impulses and inhibitions, we can approach drug treatment more effectively," Grant noted that while these findings are promising, and most people are responding to these drugs, there are still some that do not work well.

7.4 Gambling Addiction Treatment Center

Gambling addiction care is not just a matter of replacing the term "gambling" with "alcohol" or "drug" addiction and searching the Internet. Although gambling addiction is a form of impulse-control disorder and the concept of classic addiction definitely applies, the gambling addict requires specialized counseling and therapy to resolve the gambling obsession.

It will not be enough for a treatment center or hospital that is specialized only in drugs and/or alcohol. So, how do you find a treatment center for gambling addiction? here are a number of gambling addiction treatment centers in the U.S. dedicated exclusively to treating the compulsive gambler. But, they're hard to find.

The good news is that we have clinics and facilities for addiction treatment that also have what is called a gambling line, or a treatment program explicitly designed to address addiction to gambling.

Types of Treatment Programs Residential treatment services offer interdisciplinary care 24 hours a day, seven days a week, both general and advanced. Customers live at the facility and receive services from trained staff to provide specialized treatment for behavioral health problems and other related issues.

These residential treatment facilities can be in freestanding, non-hospital buildings, or in a wing of the hospital. Furthermore, residential treatment services may include homes for treating domestic violence, centers for treating non-hospital addiction, intermediate care facilities, psychiatric centers, and other non- medical arrangements.

Inpatient treatment services offer residential-like but hospital-like care. Inpatient services have as a key component the close collaboration of other service providers and entities, as to Behavioral Health Care Programs, CARF, 2002.

Regular rehabilitation exercises include patients with inhospital treatment services. The aim of care is to provide a supportive atmosphere that includes medical rehabilitation, support, addiction or mental illness treatment, and supervision.

The National Council on Problem Gambling gives a number of facilities that provide inpatient or residential gambling care. The identified facilities have offered to be included on the web, although there may also be other non-listed qualifying facilities.

The NCPG does not mean inclusion in the collection.

Aid by State the NCPG also has links to a state-by-state map as a starting point for finding help or gathering knowledge on gambling issues. In any search for an approved and accredited gambling addiction treatment center or hospital, it should be used as a starting point.

For example, the California Council on Problem Gambling (CCPG) is a non-profit organization that was founded in 1986 to support problem gamblers and their families by promoting awareness, education, research, prevention, and problem gambling treatment. It's one of the NCPG's 35 local affiliates.

The CCPG site has ties to non-California affiliates, as well as services within the state, including a directory of gambling problem counselors.

Important Factors for Assessing Treatment Center In its approach to gambling addiction treatment, not every treatment facility is the same.

 Likewise, for every person seeking help, no one form of treatment works. To be effective, gambling addiction treatment needs to be personally tailored to meet the individual client's needs.

Things to consider including the treatment setting (inpatient, outpatient, individual or group counseling, therapy, 12-stage meetings, etc.), how long the treatment program lasts, philosophical treatment approach, and the specific concerns of the gambling addict and his or her family.

Care Period The duration of care varies with each individual's needs. Clients should discuss their specific needs with the therapist. Some will be handled relatively quickly, while others may take longer, such as learning a new behavior or coping skills to handle the problems of life.

Bottom line is: do not let anything interfere with the search for professional treatment to fix a gambling problem or addiction to gambling. A lot of help is available–if you really want to overcome your gambling compulsion. It will take hard work and dedication, and years of bad behavior will not be easy to undo, but it is possible to do it.

Conclusion

Gambling problems can occur from any part of life to anyone. Your gambling ranges from a fun, harmless diversion to a serious consequence unhealthy obsession. Whether you're betting on football, scratch cards, roulette, poker, or slots — at a casino, track, or online
— a gambling problem may strain your relationships, interfere with work and cause a financial catastrophe. You might even do stuff that you never thought you'd do, like running up huge debts or even stealing gambling money.

Gambling addiction is an impulse-control condition, also known as pathological gambling, compulsive gambling or gambling disorder. If you're a compulsive gambler, even if it has negative consequences for you or your loved ones, you can't control the temptation to play. You're going to play whether you're positive or you're negative, broke or clean, and you're going to keep playing irrespective of the consequences— even if you know the odds are against you or you can't afford to lose.

Of course, without being totally out of control, you can also have a gambling problem. Any gambling activity that disrupts your life is a problem gambling. You have a gambling problem if you are obsessed with gambling, wasting more and more time and money on it, chasing losses, or gambling in spite of serious consequences in your life.

The addiction or problem with gambling is often associated with other disorders of behavior or mood. Some gamblers with problems of substance abuse, unmanaged ADHD, stress, depression, anxiety, or bipolar disorder often suffer. You will also need to tackle these and any other underlying causes to solve your gambling issues.

Although stopping gambling can sound like you're helpless, there are plenty of things you can do to solve the issue, restore your relationships and finances, and eventually regain control over your life.

References

- American Psychiatric Association, Diagnostic and Statistical Manual of Mental Disorders, American Psychiatric Association, Washington, DC, USA, 4th edition, 1994.

- G. T. Ladd and N. M. Petry, "Gender differences among pathological gamblers seeking treatment," Experimental and Clinical Psychopharmacology, vol. 10, no. 3, pp. 302–309, 2002. View at Publisher · View at Google Scholar · View at Scopus

- M. N. Potenza, M. A. Steinberg, S. D. McLaughlin, R. Wu, B. J. Rounsaville, and S. S. O'Malley, "Genderrelated differences in the characteristics of problem gamblers using a gambling helpline," The

American Journal of Psychiatry, vol. 158, no. 9, pp. 1500–1505,
2001. View at Publisher · View at Google Scholar · View at Scopus

- H. J. Shaffer, R. A. LaBrie, D. A. LaPlante, and R. C. Kidman, The Iowa Department of Public Health Gambling Treatment Services: Four Years of Evidence, Harvard Medical School, Boston Mass, USA, 2002.

- C. Guerreschi, "Le Frontiere del Gioco D'Azzardo,"

  Conferenza sul Gioco D'Azzardo Patologico, Kolpinghaus, 1998.

- G. Serpelloni, "Il Gioco d'Azzardo Patologico in Italia," The Italian Journal on Addiction, vol. 2, pp. 3–4, 2012. View at Google Scholar

- C. Villella, G. Martinotti, M. di Nicola et al., "Behavioural addictions in adolescents and young adults: results from a prevalence study," Journal of Gambling Studies, vol. 27, no. 2, pp. 203–214, 2011. View at Publisher · View at Google Scholar · View at Scopus

- American Psychiatric Association, DSM-5: Development website, 2014, http://www.dsm5.org/Pages/Default.aspx.
C. Reilly and N. Smith, "The Evolving Definition of Pathological Gambling in the DSM-5," National Center of Responsible Gaming, 2013.

- F. Angelucci, G. Martinotti, F. Gelfo et al., "Enhanced BDNF serum levels in patients with severe pathological gambling," Addiction Biology, vol. 18, no. 4, pp. 749–751, 2013. View at Publisher · View at Google Scholar · View at Scopus

- M. N. Potenza, "Neurobiology of Gambling Behaviors," ·
Current Opinion in Neurobiology, vol. 23, no. 4, p. 6607, 2013. View at Google Scholar
M. N. Potenza, "The neurobiology of pathological gambling," Seminars in clinical neuropsychiatry, vol. 6, no. 3, pp. 217–226, 2001. View at Google Scholar
· View at Scopus

- S. L. McElroy, J. I. Hudson, K. A. Phillips, P. E. Keck, and H. G. Pope, "Clinical and theoretical implications.

9 789564 025629